# Builder Sales *Power*

## A Guide for Exceptional New Home Sales PROfessionals

CHRISTINE HAMILTON

## MY DEDICATION

*"We must remember that one (sales wo)man is much the same as another, and that (s)he is best who is trained in the severest school."*

- Thucydides

I dedicate my career and life to being of service and contribution to the building industry and the world at large, fully knowing that I achieve the greatest success possible in all areas of my life when those around me win as well. I live my life as an example for others to follow and go forward with a spirit of enthusiasm, excitement and success. My life is fulfilled as I move forward with the inherent faith and belief that anything is possible and miracles do occur.

Here's to *your* success. Go. Sell. Win! You've got the POWER!

With love,
Christine Hamilton

# CONTENTS

# INTRODUCTION

It all started for me at the young, impressionable age of 18 as I was nearing graduation from high school. At that point in history, women's issues were vehemently studied and argued. Gender discrimination was all over the press and the hot topic of discussion on college campuses across the nation. Phrases like "Equal pay for equal work" and terms such as "glass ceiling" were the catchwords of the day. It was at that impressionable time in my life, within the heated sociopolitical time for women, that my mother handed me a small paperback book entitled *Sales: The Fast Track for Women* by Connie McClung Siegel. I wasn't a big reader back then, seldom choosing any books for pleasure reading, but this one piqued my interest.

Even at a time where the career options and opportunities for women were embroiled in controversy, I knew that I was going to be a *career woman*. Looking back, it is strange to think about how working as a "career woman" was the exception to the rule. It was an uncommon choice and the road less traveled by most women. Especially in the realm of sales which was considered a man's world.

Maybe it was the fascinating stories of women at the big corporations of the world like Xerox and IBM that lured me in. Or the stories of housewife turned executive and the promise of a six-figure income. It may have been the uniform style of Big Blue and their Ralph Lauren navy blue suits and crisp white button down collared shirts or the path to a shot as CEO of a multinational. More than anything, though, it was the message that performance is measured not by sexual bias but by *results*. It was this last word that resonated with me. I knew that I worked harder and excelled greater than most people. I was drawn to the idea of being compensated for my achievements. After reading Siegel's words I knew that I was destined for a career in sales!

Thus, my career in sales started just after returning from a year-long exchange to Brazil. I landed my first sales job at Swiss Colony. I remember it so clearly: I was one of those teenage girls dressed in a little red dress with embroidery stitching around the square neckline and little black apron around my waste with a bow tied at my back. I wore white knee-high socks and black slip-on clog shoes. I would stand at the storefront in Sunrise Mall offering samples of cheese and beef logs to entice customers into the store. I was hired along with 29 other girls for the Christmas season. The owner of the store, a former high school football coach, taught us a six-steps selling process. I took the six-step training to heart and at the close of the holiday season I was one of only three salespeople retained by the store. I then applied that six-step sales process to a second part-time job demonstrating facial lotion in fine department stores. I was so committed to demonstrating and discussing product uses and benefits and ringing each customer up that I was an instant success and became the top salesperson after just two months.

Though I found great success in my two part-time jobs, I wasn't content with earning minimum wage. I remembered what I read in that awesome book on sales for women, which said I could make the big bucks too. I got a job selling cars—Volkswagen and used cars to be more specific—as one of the only vehicle sales women in Sacramento and certainly the youngest at 18 years old. I was also trained by Volkswagen USA and learned the technology of automobiles and how to demonstrate a vehicle. I learned the method of flipping as well as negotiation and how to close for the immediate sale. I learned a lot about what to do and what not to do to create a pleasant buying experience for customers.

I went on to earn my Bachelor of Arts degree in social sciences with an emphasis in international political economy from the University of California at Berkeley. While at Berkeley I also gained experience in the creation of marketing materials in the university's Office of International Education, where I was responsible for helping create collateral materials, posters and fliers attract applicants to a graduate studies program in India.

Once I graduated from college, it was time for me to get a job. I landed at a company that distributed Canon copiers and facsimile machines. After a weeklong SPIN training (Situation, Problem, Implications and Needs-Payoff) at the Canon headquarters, I won a Canon wristwatch for the best demonstration of a laser fax machine. I became one of their top selling fax representatives nationwide.

During my Canon career my mother was selling real estate and doing well for herself. She lured me into her business with the promise of doubling my income. So, I got my real estate license and sold resale homes for a couple of years, becoming a top producer with RE/MAX from my very first year. But even as a resale agent, I mostly sold new homes. At that point I decided to go into new home sales. My mother directed me to Beazer Homes where, after a two-hour interview with the president of the division, I knew that the company was the one for me. I made the decision right then and there and I closed for the job in my interview. I was sent to look at some of the communities later that day and requested the one where their top sales person would be my partner.

And so it went, I went to work for Beazer Homes. The following Monday I was sent to Southern California for Charles Clarke's BOLT (Bulls, Owls, Lambs, Tiger) personality sales training. I was named Sales Rookie of the Year my first year in the home building business and won Best Salesperson of the Year for the next three consecutive years. I then earned the National Silver Award for the California and Nevada Regions and my collection of awards crescendoed with the National Association of Home Builders Gold Award for Best Salesperson for the Year.

Across my sales career, spanning multiple industries, I realized that I was purely a product of professional training. From the six step selling process I learned at Swiss Colony—I still have the notes I wrote on a tiny little spiral note pad—to my hardball experiences on the car lot... from my SPIN training at Canon to my BOLT training at Beazer... from the words of Connie Siegel to those of Dr. Stephen Covey in his book *The 7 Habits of Highly Effective People*, which I have taken to deeply in my career, I am a trained salesperson through and through. I have inculcated sales "How-To's" into the framework of my mind and my heart. They are in my greeting and my close. They are in my needs assessment and solutions offered.

The results show in my sales numbers, my income and the awards that I have received. And I chose to take the results and create a new framework in which to share them with others—to foster the Karma of my own successful career in the lives of others, just as the profound wisdom and success of my mentors influenced me.

To this day, everything I ever learned in sales is woven into the framework of my success, serving as the foundation for my mindset. And it is precisely that framework, and the mindset it depends upon, that I want to share in this book. I want you to know that you, the reader, can rely on me to offer you sound advice based on solid experience and proven by results. That is not to say that I have never lost a sale. But I used each and every loss as a learning opportunity, which partially comprises what I share with you here. I want you to learn from the culmination of my experience so you may excel in your own career, including learning from my mistakes to avoid making them yourself.

The following pages contain my very best practices and some of the habits and scripts that were the key to my success—and that will be the key to yours. So on that note, my friends, happy selling. May you be *exceptional* sales people.

# MINDSET OF A MONEYMAKER

*"Nothing can stop the (wo)man with the right mental attitude from achieving his/her goal..."*

– Thomas Jefferson

\*\*\*\*

## Attitude is Everything

And the quote continues "...nothing on earth can help the man with the wrong mental attitude." An absolute truth when it comes to success in new home sales is that attitude is everything. The thoughts and belief systems and paradigms you project onto the world around you—the way you see and perceive of the new home sales scenario—is what lays the foundation for your success more than any other single factor.

As you approach your business, you have to first know inside yourself that you have the ability to powerfully affect the marketplace. Though you cannot make the marketplace, for there are many factors much bigger than you as an individual and ultimately beyond your control, you can affect the outcome and keep those factors from becoming road blocks to your success. You must know and understand your ability to affect the marketplace—to fully accept it as your own belief, your own creed. Recognizing the interconnectedness of the universe empowers you to be a moneymaker in new home sales. You must first possess the mindset of one.

*You Can Be, Do and Have Anything!*

It's in our beingness, how we behave and what we do, the actions that we take that gets us to have anything that we want. So it all starts with our behavior. And sometimes we need to behave differently than we have in the past to achieve the results we want. Depending on who you are there may be behaviors that you may need to step into such as boldness, assertiveness, proactivity, compassion, analytical, personally responsible, worthy, trusting, open, and so forth. So if you believe that you can be do and have anything opens up the realization that you can step into new behaviors that you may be uncomfortable with, and you may take different actions than you have done in the past and you will achieve all the things you want.

### Be Personally Responsible for Results

Once you know what our "why" is, it's important to acknowledge how you are personally responsible for the results in our life. Ask yourself whether you can take that on. Seldom are we victims of circumstance. A prime example is the 1998 draft, when Payton Manning and Ryan Leaf were widely regarded as the two best players. For their rookie years, they both had horrible seasons, but when the media came to interview them on the topic, the two men acted very differently.

After a terrible third game where he completed only 1 of 15 passes, Leaf swore at a reporter and later had a meltdown on camera. After five games he had thrown nine interceptions—second-worst in the NFL. Only Peyton Manning threw more. Leaf continued to spiral downward, failing to take ownership for his performance. What did Peyton Manning say when he was interviewed? He admitted that he made a series of bad decisions. He took responsibility for his own decision-making. He took personal responsibility for his own shortfalls. He made no excuses. He did not blame others like Ryan Leaf did. He took ownership of his actions. Ryan Leaf no longer plays football, and Peyton Manning is widely considered the best quarterback in the NFL today. Do you take personal responsibility for your part in the game?

It's not necessarily enough anymore to sit back and expect marketing to bring all the traffic in. It has become the front line's job and responsibility to do what you can, what's within your sphere of influence, to bring business into the company. What can you do that may be different than what's been done already? What can you do for free or relatively inexpensively? This is just one of many areas where we can take personal responsibility for our own success and to create the desired results that we want to achieve in our lives.

One of the things that really turned a light bulb on for me was the notion of "being at cause" for our own experiences in life. Notice I'm using the word "at cause" and not fault or blame. Let's just say, for example, that you've had a negative interaction with a family member or a customer. Instead of asserting that the other person did something or is wrong, turn that mirror right back around and acknowledge that, at the very least, you may have had an "at cause" role. Be gut-level honest with yourself. What ways did you affect the other person? Remember, we are all connected. We are all like one. In what way were you at cause? Again, it does not mean fault or blame. You have to take responsibility for your part in the game, you have to recognize how your choices come to bear on your life. So you want to choose wisely, of course. You want to choose positive outcomes.

When you really accept this notion about being personally responsible and acknowledging how you're at cause for your own experience, you realize that it's extremely empowering. I used to get emails from corporate during the downturn asking, *"How are you doing it? I notice your sales numbers are really high...what are you doing to keep up the pace?"* because my team was consistently making sales, even outside of promotional periods. I used to respond with my belief that we can powerfully affect the marketplace. Are we market makers? No, but we can powerfully affect it.

That's how much strength I believe you have inside of you. With the right choices, the right actions and the right decisions, you will bring back sales and profit and happy customers. If that's what you put out, that's exactly what should get back. So always hold yourself—not your boss or your company, not your family or friends, but yourself—

responsible for the results in your life. After all, results are really the only objective way to measure people's effectiveness, especially in business.

## Be PROactive

To support your moneymaking mindset and perpetuate the wellbeing of your business, proactivity is the greatest source of sustenance. Being a PROactive PROfessional means consistently doing what you have to do to keep business coming into the company so you can consistently close sales.

### Use Your "R" and "I"

When it comes to being proactive, your "R" and Your "I" are two of the best, most effective tools you have at your disposal: resources and initiative. You know what resources you have, and you are the sole bearer of your own initiative. If you aren't achieving the results you need or want, ask yourself, "*What can I do? Who do I know that can help me? How can I make this happen? What else can I do differently?*"

Ask yourself these questions regularly, and use your resources and initiative to carry you throughout the year to set yourself apart from the competition. For example, there may be certain times of the year, such as the holiday season, when you find the market (and your competition) slowing down. Rather than acquiescing to the "slower time of year," use the inactivity of others as a barometer for increased activity on your part. Step up your game! Sales can happen most every day of the year if you behave proactively and prepare using any and all resources at your disposal. Strive to get more than your "fair share" of the pie. Rather than settling for the pace of slower seasons, be proactive and employ your resources and initiative to consistently bring in the business, to consistently make sales and more importantly, to consistently close sales. Consistency is the key! It's your own proactivity that makes you consistent.

As the famous football coach Lou Holtz said, "How you respond to the challenge in the second half will determine what you become after the game, whether you are a winner or a loser." Consider selling homes today like the second half of the game, where the first half was the real estate boom and you now find yourself in the current marketplace.

How you choose to respond is going to determine whether you win sales or you don't. Those who are proactive recognize that *how* they respond to any market condition or any challenge is a matter of choice. Choose to be a winner. It is manufacturing the results you want, for yourself, for your business. Being a PROactive PROfessional will far-and-away set you apart from all the competition.

**** 

## 100% Rule

*As I mentioned in the introduction, after I graduated from high school and returned from my foreign exchange to Brazil, I got my very first job in sales working for a company called Swiss Colony, selling a variety of cheeses, beef logs and gift baskets. In that very first sales job, I learned an invaluable lesson that became embedded in my professional mindset forever more. The owner of the franchise had what he called the "100% Rule." The 100% Rule is plain and simple: Do your 100% best job, with every customer, always, every time, without fail.*

*At 18 years old, I wrote that edict down on a little notepad. It is something I live by to this day and pass on to others. In every professional venture since, the 100% Rule has been inculcated in my own mindset. Working and living the 100% Rule brought me great success in sales. The bar is 100%. It is the standard to which I hold myself and others accountable. As Madeline Bridges said, "Give your best and the best will come back to you".*

****

## Unique Opportunity

Within the 100% Rule is an implicit statement regarding the value of each and every customer. Each and every customer who comes to your sales center is a unique opportunity. Think about what the notion of a unique opportunity means… no moment or opportunity will ever be an exactly replicated, no conditions will lend themselves to an exact repeat. The same applies to customers who come to your sales centers, to any interaction with any potential customer. Each customer is a unique opportunity. Never bank on the "be back bus".

It is imperative that you, as a New Home Sales PROfessional, know that you will never have another opportunity to affect a person's home-buying experience. You never know if you will see or hear from a customer again. In fact, be back traffic accounts for only 10-15% of the building industry's return visitors. Therefore, regard every interaction as a one-time shot. Maintain that mindset and you will commit to yourself that make the most of every customer opportunity.

## The POWER and Value of a Handshake

Part of making the most of every opportunity is recognizing what it is that any given customer needs or wants. As explained in *The Five Love Languages*, written by Dr. Gary Chapman, people understand love—and not necessarily romantic love, but love in the sense of human warmth—brotherly and sisterly love—when it is expressed through one of five ways: words of affirmation, quality time, receiving gifts, acts of service, or physical touch. Though each of these five languages is potentially applicable to any individual, it is physical touch that can take the smallest form while making the biggest difference in a customer's decisions.

Physical touch triggers the release of endorphins in the brain, encouraging an individual's confidence and comfort. There is a key exchange of energy when you shake another's hand, and yet typically only 25% of new home salespeople do it. It is a simple, direct way to

6

immediately connect with an individual, to begin to build a relationship with a customer from the outset. It is an effective icebreaker.

By beginning your greetings with a warm, sincere, professional handshake, your customers are more likely to be open with their sharing their needs, wants, desires, and the current living situation that is prompting them to visit your sales center. Additionally, when you take a moment to reach out and shake hands with a customer, you have the immediate benefit of getting a sense for your customer's personality. A person's handshake—the grip, motion, length of time that goes into it—can tell you immediately someone's personality type, which will tell you what kind of behavior you need to adopt in relating to and working with that individual.

Not only do you benefit by gaining insight into your customer's character, but a handshake allows the customer to benefit from getting to know you. You represent your builder and the value and quality that your builder has to offer. Extending your hand demonstrates your professionalism and compassion. It is a simple way to put customers at ease while establishing a level of transparency which allows them to feel like they are in good hands. A handshake is also a great opportunity to establish eye contact, which is one of the most important components of customer interaction. Eye contact is often overstated but way underestimated as a critical component of establishing a meaningful and trusting relationship with a customer.

It is crucial to remember that every manner of pre-sale customer service bespeaks the builder—its quality and value. By extending your hand you professionally establish yourself, your homes and your company as the best in the marketplace.

## Unparalleled Customer Service

Having a customer centered mindset isn't just about differentiating yourself from the competition by being the best that you can be through your words and actions. This means extending unparalleled customer service to every individual who walks through your doors. Make it your mission to create the best buying experience for your customers.

As the New Home Sales PROfessional, you have the power to establish the context. You also have the opportunity—and responsibility—to guide the experience in a superbly positive direction for the customer. As the builder's front line, it is you who sets the tone and who helps the customer have a positive experience. And a positive customer experience is all you need to transform one sales center visit to one new home sale. Whomever said that buying a home is one of the most stressful experiences in life was mistaken. The question is what actions can you take starting now to improve the customer experience you are creating?

## Be Open

You only need one: one buyer, one sale to make a difference in your business. That is why your mind must be open to every single prospect that walks through your doors. Treat each and every customer as though he or she is your only one. Shed yourself of judgment and stereotype and approach each and every person with equal opportunity. In Malcolm Gladwell's book *Blink: The Power of Thinking Without Thinking*, he explores the idea of "thin-slicing," which describes how we all make snap judgments about others. In new home sales, it is important to maintain a mindset of being open to every single person as a potential customer.

When someone walks through the doors of your sales center, carefully reflect upon your immediate thought process. Ask yourself whether you are sizing up the individual based on their physical or material aspects. Do your initial questions focus on qualifying or disqualifying your prospects. Rather than opting toward either, simply be open to the individual. Assume that every single person you encounter in your sales center wants to buy. Look for ways and reasons that they can and will buy...today.

Think first and foremost that every single person needs a home to live in. Second, regardless if he or she is able to buy at the moment, anyone can qualify to buy in the future. You never know until you get deep into the specifics—until you ask the tough questions and dare to dig—whether you have what the customer needs. Look for how you can help them move forward rather than whether they are willing and able. They are willing given the proper set of circumstances. They are able one way or another. You need to find and/or create the set of circumstances. You need to show them the way.

## Believe Customers Can, Will and Do BUY on the FIRST Visit

If you provide unparalleled customer service, set the context for a phenomenal home-buying experience, and recognize the value of each and every customer, you may find that customers can, will, and do buy on their first visit—much more than you may expect. Take a moment to notice your own reactions to this paradigm. Do you believe that people can, will and do buy on first visit? Or are you entertaining all the reasons how and why they can't?

Notice if you are focused on the obstacles to buying now. Are you willing to adjust your frame of mind and seriously consider how and why people would want and be able to move forward immediately? If you can find the will and the way for people to buy immediately, apply that expectation to your mindset and recognize that your responsibility is to unveil and magnify a customer's reasons for buying right there, at that moment, that day. Just like you have different reasons for selling a home in a day, each customer has different reasons for looking at, and buying, a home in a day. Always drive for the sale today. You never know what unique opportunities may present themselves. You will find customers who say, "*YES!*" right now.

## Be Urgency

*As a Sales PROfessional, I learned the value of selling people in the ways they want and need to be sold when I was challenged one day to sell a button to a stranger on the street. My only guideline was that I could not sell the button on the main street. I had recently written a book so I decided to try and find a bookstore where I could speak with the manager about my book and as an extension of that conversation ask him or her to buy my button.*

*I walked a few blocks and asked a couple where the closest bookstore was. We started talking and I asked questions about where they were from and what they were doing in town, and I explained to them that I was trying to find a bookstore to sell my button. I asked if they were interested and they inquired as to how much. I asked, "What would you give me?" and they responded they'd pay five dollars, so I sold the button right then and there. The catch was that I had broken the rule and sold it on the main street.*

*The next day I was tasked with selling another button, only this time I had to do so within 15 minutes. I saw one guy briskly walking down the street so I caught up with him and asked him if he'd like to buy my button, to which he responded that he would but didn't have any money. He said he was on his way to an ATM and would come back. I told him I had a limited amount of time and asked if he'd be back within 10 minutes, at which point he told me I should find another customer.*

*I then saw a woman hurriedly unloading a van. I approached her and asked if I could help, to which she said yes because she was running late. I said "Great, let's go!" and immediately began helping her unload her van. When we finished I explained to her my situation and asked, "Would you like to buy my button?" to which she responded by asking how much I wanted for it. Instead of asking, "What would you pay for it?" as I had done the day before I asked, "What's the maximum value you would give it?" "Twenty bucks," she exclaimed. I sold my button for more than the day before and returned on time.*

*The two valuable lessons this experience taught me were to help people the way they want to be helped and you will hit their "hot button" reason for buying today, and that urgency has everything to do with the buying and selling process.*

## Be Committed

One last aspect of cultivating the mindset of a moneymaker is a strong individual commitment to continuing education and personal development. Always be on the lookout for opportunities to learn and grow. Attend seminars, take classes, read and listen to audio books—do whatever works for you to grow personally, stay amped up and in a sales-oriented mindset.

Personal development can be instrumental in uncovering the beliefs and biases that are holding you back from realizing what you truly want. Overall, big results come from a commitment to combining effective techniques with getting past any paradigms that prevent you from achieving what you say you want. Your relationships with your friends, family, coworkers, managers and customers will improve. The more you become a better person, the more you become a better *salesperson*.

## Recap

• When it comes to being a moneymaker in this business, your attitude is everything. Adopt a positive stance and put your resources and initiative to use as a PROactive PROfessional.

• Remember the 100% Rule: Do your 100% best job, with every customer, always, every time, without fail.

• Be open to every customer who walks in your sales center, and regard each customer as a unique, viable sales opportunity. Extend unparalleled customer service each and every time, and always drive for the sale on the first day.

• Make a habit of continuing education and personal development. It will make you a better person and a better salesperson.

## Crucial Questions

• "What can I do?"
• "What else can I do with what I have?"
• "What resources are available to me?"
• "Who do I know that can help me?"
• "How can I make this happen?"

# FINDING YOUR WHY

*"If you have a 'why' of life, you can bear any 'how'."*
– Friedrich Nietzsche

*"Our deepest fear is not that we are inadequate. Our deepest fear is that we are powerful beyond measure."*
– Marianne Williamson

****

*When I worked as a frontline sales professional, I recall a time when our vice president of sales asked all the salespeople to submit their goals for the year. The number I wrote down was $200,000. Afterward, I kicked myself for having submitted that figure. I kicked myself because I held back what was really wanted to earn. What I honestly had in mind was to earn $300,000 that year. But I was afraid to admit it to my boss. I lied because I feared he would think I was being too greedy. I was also afraid that the other salespeople would resent me for being assigned to the best communities. I feared that they would complain to the boss and that I might get reassigned to a different, less desirable community. So, regretfully, I submitted a more modest goal.*

*Not long after, I attended a company sales training event. While there, I couldn't shake the feeling that I had sold myself short. So, I shared with the sales trainer how I felt and the truth about my $300,000 goal. She encouraged me to stick to the higher number. That year I ended up making over $330,000! Selling myself short was one of the* *biggest mistakes I made as a frontline salesperson. Instead of believing in my own goal, I was focused on the possible judgment of others. I reduced myself because I feared what others might think. That's a mistake! The good news is you have the opportunity to learn from my mistakes. Conclusion: Embrace your greatness and go for what you really want!*

\*\*\*\*

## Sales Motivation: Find Your *Why*

One of the keys to a successful mindset as a New Home Sales PROfessional is identifying what it is that motivates you personally. Your aspirations will most likely be different than your company sales goals. Ask yourself, *"How much money do I want to make?"* and then stretch yourself to identify why. Finding your *why* is the most effective way to stay motivated. You must be completely clear on why you are doing what you are doing. You must ask yourself what is driving you to make the sale today.

What I have found is that most people are really motivated for their own reasons, and not necessarily for builders' reasons. Each person on the front line is motivated by what is in it for them—or their "why"—and that comes with a myriad of reasons. The key is to become very clear about what is driving you because whatever you do in life affects the world and the people you leave by behind for years. The vision of your purpose, your why, is what powers your goals and gives meaning to your accomplishments. As Paulo Coelho stated, *"A life without a cause is a life without effect."* Always know that it is in your power to choose and realize your desired outcome. What effect do you want to have?

## Four Steps to Realizing Your Goals

There are four important steps you must perform in order to realize your goals: Clarify, Write, Envision, and Act. Each step is a milestone toward your goal-oriented journey, helping you to gain and maintain momentum toward what you want.

## *Want vs. Would Like*

A great way to begin finding your *why*—and achieving your dreams—is determining whether your motivation hinges on something you really *want,* or something you simply *would like.* What you want is that which you are willing to do what it takes to get. This is a critical distinction in defining your goals because your *wants* will take you inestimably farther in your success than that which you *would-like* ever can. Do not agree to a goal with yourself if you are not truly willing to do what it takes to achieve it. Sometimes it will require you stepping out of your comfort zone and *be*having differently.

## *Step 1: Clarify*

Before you can undertake any course of action, it is imperative that you get clear with yourself about what it is that you really want. What is it that you are shooting for? A home in the hills or a new sports car? To get out of debt or prepare for retirement? To provide for you family or pay for your children's college tuition? To pay off your mortgage or travel? Or do you want to do more at church or to be able to make financial contributions to your favorite causes? At this juncture, take the time to think about and make the distinction between what you *want* and what you *would-like.* For example, if someone gave you lottery tickets for your birthday, you may like to win the lottery. It could be a pleasant, unexpected windfall profit that you didn't have to work for. But unless you're buying tickets yourself, it probably isn't something you really want.

The key difference between the two is that a *would-like* is a matter of convenience or a nice perk, whereas a *want* is something for which you are willing to do what it takes to get! This is where your "willpower" lies. The question is what are you willing to do?

*True to You*

No one else can give you the answer to your *why*. Being true to yourself about your *wants* and *would-likes* will make all the difference in your ability to achieve. Ask yourself, *"Is this something I want for myself or what somebody else wants for me?"* Sometimes it helps to ask such reflective questions as, *"Am I being the person I want to be? Am I doing the things I want to do? Do I have the things I want to have?"* Understanding whether you are acting of your own accord or out of obligation to another is an important thing to discern when it comes to your why. Know what are your choices—your own life choices. Before you can find success in sales, you have to get clear on what you want for yourself and why you want it for yourself. Only then will you be internally driven to do what it takes to make enough sales to get what you want. Once you are clear on your intentions, the methods for how to achieve your goals will become apparent.

## S.M.A.R.T. Goals

Establishing goals using the S.M.A.R.T. pillars is a great way to ensure that your goals are truly reflective of your aspirations and abilities. Though the mnemonic has been adapted over time, the term serves as a guide for developing criteria by which to set objectives. Each tenet term signifies a point of consideration when defining and outlining your goals. The **S** stands for *specific*, **M** for *measurable*, **A** for *attainable*, **R** for *risky*, and **T** for *timeline*.

*Specific*: Being specific about your goal is important because it orients you in a distinct direction with a clear focus. Whether it is earning more than you did last year, for example or something else, establish specifically what it is you want to achieve. This will better allow you to track and acknowledge your own progress.

*Measurable*: Part of tracking your progress toward a goal is making that goal measurable. Rather than just saying, *"I want to earn more this year,"* express yourself in more well-defined terms. Take the specific direction you established and put a dollar amount to it: *"I want to make*

*$50,000 more this year than I did last year, for a total of $200,000.*" You have to explicitly state what it is you're working toward.

*Attainable*: It is important to set your sights high, but never give yourself a goal that is not attainable in reality. For example, don't establish a sales figure of $300,000 this year if, stationed in the exact same community, you earned $60,000 last year; or, don't assert that you will sell 300 homes this year if your company only built 60 last year. Take stock of past precedents and future opportunities to create goals that are within your reach—if you stretch!

*Risky*: While your goals should be attainable, they should also cause you to stretch yourself. Don't resign yourself to goals that are small or easy. Push yourself to do more than you have in the past . As you think about how you want to define your goal, reflect on your maximum potential. Ask yourself whether your goals are moving you toward realizing your potential as a person and a professional.

*Timeline*: You always want to set a timeline for your goals. The timeline serves as a framework for all the other components: allowing you to be more specific, providing an extra way to ensure your goals are measurable, giving context for what is attainable, and anticipating how your goal is risky. Setting timelines for your goals creates a means to access your forward progress.

*Step 2: Write them down*

Once you've clarified what it is you *want*, write it down. Write it down in a place where you can return to it and where it will serve as a ready reminder to you at all times. Not only write down your goals for what you want, but write down the other aspects you uncovered: your motivations for wanting it, how it falls within the S.M.A.R.T. guidelines, and what it will take to get it.[*]

---

[*] If you would like to discuss your goals with me or if you would like a free worksheet to help you clarify what you want, please call (916) 768-5525.

When you write out your goals, you are in actuality making an outward, open assertion and staking a claim for yourself. Use this as an opportunity to again explore your personal *why*. As Friedrich Nietzsche said, "He who has a *why* in life can bear almost any *how*."

For many people, money—and, more importantly, what money can buy—is the driving force. Perhaps you want to be debt-free and be able to do whatever you desire in life and have peace of mind. Perhaps you want to purchase a new home, or pay off the one you currently have mortgaged. Or maybe you want to travel and enjoy the luxuries of life while you're still young enough to appreciate them. You may want to buy a sports car you've always yearned for or some other personal reward. Or you may just want to be able to spend time with your family—and to provide for your family more thoroughly by having the necessary financial resources to pay for college tuition or other needs. At the end of the day, perhaps you just want to be able to retire and want to ensure that you have the liquefiable assets that will enable you to live comfortably in retirement.

Another driving force behind people's goals is recognition. You may just want to be recognized for your hard work and contribution to your industry and to the community. Perhaps you have a vision of yourself and what your life will look like, and bringing that vision to life is your motivation. Or maybe you are not motivated by recognition, but rather by an ability to give back to the community or industry. Your goal may be to donate to or support different causes, whether it is church or a building industry-related charity like HomeAid or Ronald McDonald House. Your goal could simply be to provide for others who are less fortunate, or underrepresented, or in need in some way. All of these reasons are worthy and only you can say what matters most to you. The *why* is where you will find the emotion behind your reason. Tap into your '*why*'. If you have a reason for reaching a goal, create a way to do it and you will surely have the effect on the world that you wish to have.

When you find your reason, write it down and put a dollar amount or other such figure to it. Make it measurable. Remember not to discount or reduce the number you really want. The first thought that comes to your mind is the best thought. Do not worry about the judgment of others. You are not greedy for wanting more for yourself. Take that first thought and put together your timeline, creating for yourself something that is attainable while remaining risky enough to push your potential. Write it down and read it regularly so that it is in your mind every single day.

## Step 3: Visualize

In addition to writing down your goals, keep them in a place that is regularly visible to you. Part of defining a goal, and what it will mean to achieve it, is visualizing what the end result looks like to you . In his landmark book *The 7 Habits of Highly Effective People*, Dr. Stephen Covey lists as his second habit, "Begin with the end in mind." So, begin your pursuit with what you want in mind. What will the end look like, feel like, be like; what will it enable; what will it mean for you?

Envisioning what you want doesn't have to be limited to reading a list and seeing it in your own mind. Consider also creating a vision board and use pictures to illustrate what you want.

As you do so, always leave space for the universe to provide more and better than you expected. When you envision your goals, try not to place finite boundaries around them. If your goal is to make $100,000, say to yourself, "*I want to make $100,000 **or more** this year.*" Beyond the hard work you put in each day to achieve your goals, cultivate an abundant mentality that is open to receive. Be open to achieving more than you initially desired.

Paulo Coelho, author of *The Alchemist*, is attributed the expression "When a person really desires something, all the universe conspires to help that person to realize his dream." Go back to the question of what you really want and how you will get it. As with any goal or dream, there will be obstacles to be sure—the universe will inevitably test you and challenge you to see if you are in pursuit of something you simply would like or of something you really want. The universe will test your determination to see if you're really willing to do what it takes to reach your goal. In the end, the way you achieve the results you want in life may not necessarily happen in the way you anticipated. That's why you must always remain open to the universe providing for you. Watch for opportunities that will support you in moving forward.

*Step 4: Take Action Now*

The final step—after you clarify, write down, and visualize your ideas—is to act on them. In believing that you will get back from the universe what you put in, know that you are responsible for the results you garner in life. Ask yourself what you can do to bring business in and act immediately. What can you do to make sales happen? Do your best job with every person who comes through your sales center and be proactive about what the end result will look like.

Don't get too caught up in devising a plan or determining exactly how you are going to reach your goal, but be prepared to take positive action right away. Ideas will come to you as long as you are absolutely clear about what you want and why. Practice awareness. Ideas may flash into your mind at any given moment. Be prepared to receive those moments and take action.

An important aspect of being able to take action is to protect yourself against negativity. Don't partake in information or practices or partnerships that will depress or discourage you in any way.

\*\*\*\*

*In 2007, I returned to the housing industry after taking almost five years off during the boom to start a family. My salespeople would complain to me, "Oh, it's just not the same. It's so tough out there." After our first couple of sales meetings, I felt beat up, slumped over under the weight of all their negativity. Finally I decided I couldn't—I wouldn't—listen to it anymore. It dawned on me that when people project negative energy and attitude, it affects the others around them. the following sales meeting, I told my team, "No more negativity in our meetings." From there on out, our discussions and exchange of information were only positive in nature. It made a world of difference in the spirit of all of us.*

Your goals are yours alone. Protect and honor your personal space from anything that may adversely affect the dreams you build within.

In the words of Dr. Robert Schuller, *"You can go anywhere from where you are—if you are willing to dream big and work hard."* As you conceive your goals, enact your goals, and achieve your goals, don't forget to take a long view of your career by updating your goals as you go. Refer to your written goals and gauge how you are doing. Are you on the right track or do you need to make adjustments to catch up? Are you slightly ahead of your game and want to consider adjusting your goals upward? Never forget to dream big and work hard—and also to plan S.M.A.R.T. It begins with you and what is in your head and in your heart. All you need to do is start.

## Recap

• Don't sell yourself short. Stick to your dreams.

• Find your *why*. It is the means to the end, whatever that may be for *you*. Remember to discern between *wants* and *would-likes*.

• When it comes to your internal motivation and your sales goal, use your S.M.A.R.T. tenets—ensure that your goal is specific, measurable, attainable, risky and that there is a timeline attached.

• After you've clarified your S.M.A.R.T. goals, follow the remaining three steps: Write, Envision, and Act. Creating a vision board of your goals and let the images work on you.

• Update your goals so as not to lose sight of your progress, and to encourage yourself toward greatness.

## Crucial Questions

- "How much money do I want to make?"
- "What do I want versus what I would like? What is my why?"

- "Is this something I want for myself or what somebody else wants for me?
- "Am I being the person I want to be? Am I doing the things I want to do? Do I have the things I want to have?"
- "What can I do to make the sales happen?"
- "Am I on track with my S.M.A.R.T. goals?"
- "Am I willing to do what it takes?"

# BRINGING IN THE BUSINESS

*"If you give a man a fish you feed him for a day. If you teach a man to fish you feed him for a lifetime."*

*– Lao Tzu*

****

*One Saturday during the middle of the day, I was on a coaching call with a woman who was seeking my help with her business. At one point I notice that we have been on the phone for about 90 minutes, and I realize that we were not interrupted once—not once—by her customers. For the time of day and day of the week, that indicated to me a problem. I commented on my observation and she confirmed that no one had come in.*

*It was then that I decided we needed to shift the focus of our discussion to not being a victim of slow business, instead identifying what was within her sphere of influence to bring business into the company. She quickly realized that it does not help to complain about business, or marketing, or anything else. She was the only one who could make herself unstoppable. And she could be unstoppable by adopting the mindset of a moneymaker.*

****

## Stepping Up Your Game

In today's new home sales environment, it's no longer enough to sit back in our sales centers and wait for marketing to bring us traffic. The rules of the game have changed. The question is whether or not you are changing and growing with the market. It's time to step up your game!

There is an essential frame of mind for today's Marketing and Sales PROfessional seeking to bring in the business for his or her company. It requires hard work and continuous learning within a marketplace that is constantly changing. As with any supply-and-demand business cycle, the conditions expand and contract. Finding success is not only about establishing goals but also about finding innovative ways to achieve those goals.

A response-able approach means choosing your response to today's marketplace—making the market a better place by making some changes within yourself as a sales PROfessional. Stepping up your game is about doing more with less and emphasizing what *you* can do to affect growth within your business. It's about generating your own leads and traffic. It is about taking personal responsibility for your effort and your results, regardless of the market climate.

It is important to step out and generate business from beyond your desk at your sales office. Your computers won't make the sales for you. You have got to go out and be live. In the words of Goethe, "Whatever you do, or dream you can, begin it. Boldness has genius and power and magic in it."

## Best Practices

A sure way to step up your game and bring in the business is to abide by two best practices aimed at maximizing your exposure to customers and engaging potential new homebuyers in personal, demonstrative ways. Each of these practices will help generate traffic to your communities at little to no cost, effectively allowing you to do more business without overextending your time or resources.

*#1: Conduct Presentations*

One of the most effective things you can do when it comes to bringing in business to your company is conduct live presentations. The first part of this is choosing where to conduct your presentations. At the outset, it is always easier to go to other people rather than challenging them to come to you. You will almost always find a presentation to be more effective, and an audience to be more responsive, if you place yourself in their environment.

Real estate offices are critically important venues for new home sales. After all, realtors are the ones who present ready business through their relationships with potential buyers. They know the markets, they know the needs and wants of their clients, and they are the ones who identify options for uniting those two entities. By presenting in real estate offices, you place yourself at the forefront of realtors' minds. This yields great potential for the information you share with the realtors to be further shared with their clients.

But real estate offices are also obvious—a given, in a certain sense. Chances are, you already pay brokers who bring their clients to your community. There is an embedded reciprocal relationship there that doesn't necessarily lend itself to *new and untapped* business opportunities and relationships. The solution: take your presentations to unexpected places. In the words of Ovid, *"Let your hook always be cast; in the pool where you least expect it, there will be fish."* There are countless venues with ready, captive audiences willing to receive your time and attention such as Rotary and Toastmasters clubs; automobile dealerships that have weekly meetings; suppliers, vendors and other industry affiliates whose products are used in your homes; the chamber of commerce for your locality and more. Chances are these organizations are willing to allow you to come and do an educational presentation—all you have to do is ask.

In addition to live, in-person presentations, you should also be willing to present live on the Web. At a time when the world is more intertwined than ever, take advantage of that connectedness. Just as with seeking opportunities in unexpected venues, an online presence can extend your reach to additional audiences. Today, many people enjoy the comfort of being able to do almost anything from their homes. Structuring your presentations in webinar allows you to reach people without asking them to come to you or having to go to them. It also enables you to create series of presentations tailored to different topic areas that suit different audiences—for example, the amenities in your community; your community's location and proximity to schools, shopping and entertainment centers; your floor plans and in-home features; or loan programs for new home purchases. By tapping into digital venues as well as physical ones, you're able to send out information that will surely bring in business. Where you conduct a presentation, though, is only the first half of the equation. The second is *how* you conduct a presentation.

Ask yourself what a really good live presentation really looks like. Most average new home sales people take a conventional approach—occasionally visiting real estate offices with a stack of fliers, perhaps bringing edible treats for the office or the promise of a giveaway. Most likely, the typical professional will do a quick pitch about his or her community, hand out fliers and then head out. But is that truly impressive? Is it powerful or affecting or influential? Does it do anything to demonstrate the value and quality of your homes and builder?

**\*\*\*\***

*When I worked for Beazer Homes, a top-10 homebuilder in the U.S., I would assemble a team of three—typically including myself, the new homes information manager, and one of the sales professionals—and we would venture out to the real estate offices surrounding our community and any other venue that would say "Yes" to a presentation. We'd dress in our matching company shirts—a red polo or more formal white button-down each with the company logo—and black pants or skirts, and would show up looking sharp, in-sync and energized. Each team member would take the opportunity to introduce himself or herself and the team would offer a succinct discussion of our ABCs, or Area, Builder and Community.*

*What set our presentations apart from all others was that we would bring display items for products used in our homes. Using these display items, we would actively demonstrate the features to better illustrate their benefits. We'd bring in a display box of a Zurn plumbing manifold from our homes to show how it creates a home run, which is a direct line, to each individual fixture in the house. The direct line reduces the time it takes to receive hot water at each individual fixture. Additionally, it allows you to turn water off to individual fixtures instead of the entire house. We'd also bring our LP Techshield radiant barrier box to demonstrate how the radiant-barrier roof sheathing in our homes reduces attic temperatures by up to 30 degrees and reflects radiant heat back into the attic in winter. Without fail, our product demonstrations were more impressive and garnered greater interest in our homes than any broker luncheon ever could. This was how we demonstrated value and quality and taught others about our homes.*

****

The point is to inform and educate others. Empower them. That is the key to a great presentation. Consider the features of a home that may go unnoticed by potential buyers but that could give you an edge in their decision-making process. For example, direct runs in a plumbing system can reduce water waste by thousands of gallons a year. Radiant-barrier roof sheathing can prevent a substantial amount of heat from permeating an attic. Not only do both these features promote energy efficiency, as a result they also result in significant financial savings for the homeowner. By presenting these features—offering tangible samples with which you can show true function—you build greater associations for your customers with regard to how a home's features can benefit them. Such demonstrations allow you to elaborate on the quality of your homes while building trust and confidence with agents and your future homeowners.

It is important to note, too, that presentations don't have to be limited by the availability of display items. Go through your homes as they are being built and take photos of the features and structure. Place these photos within a polished PowerPoint presentation and bring it along on your visits to other organizations to offer the audience an immersive, first-hand experience. You don't have to have a model on hand to illustrate how the warranty on Moen plumbing fixtures even includes the finish, for example. Whatever the form of your presentation, the most important factor is ensuring it is informative and educational. That is what will set you and your builder apart from other salespeople and their company.

Most builders aren't conducting presentations across diverse audiences much less professionally and systematically demonstrating their products and components used in their homes. Even if your homes are built like every other builder's—and the majority of new homes are very comparable—going out and demonstrating the value and quality of your homes will prove your value and give you the competitive advantage time after time.

Informing and educating others builds the perceived value and quality of the homes you sell. The payoff is increased market share and increased sales, closings and commissions. Conducting presentations is the singularly most effective practice, in terms of results and costs, imaginable in today's new home sales arena. Don't give them fish, or lunch. Teach them to fish. As you teach others to fish, you feed and empower them for a lifetime. By feeding them for a lifetime, you feed yourself and your company for a lifetime. That's how it works. [*]

*#2: Leveraging Others*

A standard real estate office visit may interest brokers in your home for the moment, but dynamic presentations conducted across a range of people and places will teach people about how your homes are constructed and provide them with knowledge and understanding of your product that is lasting. By playing to diverse audiences—visiting different types of organizations and delivering powerfully informative content—you cast a larger net in terms of the interest you may capture.

---

[*] If you would like coaching on your live or online presentations, please call (916) 768-5525. There is no cost to you.

For some new home salespeople, presenting to different audiences may be a significant personal obstacle. To overcome this, situate yourself within a team where you can build a sense of camaraderie and have the support you need to feel comfortable while delivering an engaging presentation. Or, if you are presenting solo, think back to your personal goals and recognize your opportunity to achieve. Step up your game and feel emboldened by the potential of today's marketplace. In an industry where everyone's options have been economized, you must be your own most effective and least expensive, tool.

Part of bringing in the business is positioning yourself in front of people who will spread the word about what you have to say. If people are impressed, they will tell others—guaranteed. And the more people you reach, the more your business will grow. In his book *The Tipping Point: How Little Things Can Make a Big Difference*, author Malcolm Gladwell explores the phenomenon of something small crossing a threshold into large-scale attention or acclaim.

Never be afraid to put yourself out there and ask for referrals. That is how you can create a tipping point for your new home sales. At every opportunity, you have to remember to leverage the attention of those you are engaging with such that your word will spread and business will grow exponentially. Three core opportunities to create leverage are by networking, building your database, and picking up the telephone.

Networking

Networking provides another significant opportunity to engage others and leverage them to sing your praises and bring you business. One of the most common mistakes people make in networking endeavors is to subsist on the same contacts, circulating within the same realms. To make a difference in your business, you have got to explore less charted areas and make new acquaintances.

For each and every networking event you attend, set yourself a goal for how many people you are going to connect with—to have a real conversation with. Within each conversation, prioritize the other person.

Find out who they are, what they are about, where they are in life. Establish the conditions for an interpersonal relationship. This will lead you to know how they stand in terms of a home and what you may be able to offer.

After making a new connection and exchanging business cards, follow up with him or her by sending a brief *"Nice to meet you"* email within that same day of making the acquaintance. It is never too soon to cultivate the relationship. The next step is to add each and every contact you make to your social networks and your email distribution list. Maximize your profiles, memberships, and automated email campaigns to work for you.

Building Your Database

There should be a clear-cut goal, a crystallized intention, across all aspects of your business. At the end of every presentation or networking event, you must always be building your database.

While you are out on the front lines engaging your market and uncovering new customers, your database will always be there—helping you communicate and promote your business through email campaigns and other marketing functions. In order to effectively extend your outreach, track your starting point—that is how many contacts you currently have and measure its growth.

When you visit real estate offices or other organizations, collect as many business cards as you can. As you meet and exchange information with individuals, get a feel for who are the POIs: People of Influence. The term POI describes any individual who influences a large number of people, such as the manager of a large team within an organization. Often the database of a POI precipitates to hundreds if not thousands of other contacts. By ingratiating yourself into the professional circle of a POI, you grant yourself new opportunities for exposure and dissemination of your message.

Another type of person worth getting to know, as Gladwell discusses in *The Tipping Point*, is the maven—generally described as a trusted expert in a particular field who seeks to pass knowledge on to others.

Mavens differ from POIs in that they may not influence a substantial number of people under them but, because of their knack for gathering information, they often are the first to pick up on new trends. Their personality is driven by a desire to talk and promote. Their popularity typically extends in online forums and beyond where they can engage with friends and family, contribute membership to groups, and post discussions across social media platforms. You will find that different contacts bring different benefits to your business.

To ensure your database remains robust, you must be vigilant about capturing the contacts you make. Beyond interpersonal interactions, think of the more inert ways to collect data, such as guest registration cards or visitor surveys conducted within your new homes community. It is not unusual for these data points to become lost leads, languishing at the bottom of someone's bag or left in a desk drawer. Transferring that information into your business's database is imperative and should be a firm expectation.

Get those leads in your database and, in doing so, use them to determine the effectiveness of your efforts. Results are the surest way to measure your success. Build your database and you will bring in the business.

## Picking Up the Phone

Besides your sheer courage, charm and determination, the telephone still remains your most effective tool when it comes to making contact, maintaining relationships, and bringing in the business. Every single person entered into your database should receive a phone call from you, and should receive one while the interaction is still fresh. Presentations always prompt questions and considerations in audience members, though circumstances don't always allow for in-depth discussion.

Instead of letting peoples' interest go untapped, call your new contacts as soon as possible—while the information is still at the surface of their minds, while they are still open to what you have to say. Do not waste time and do not settle for sending blanket emails to contacts with whom you have personally engaged.

Potential customers want to feel heard and understood. Call them and show them that you care. Find out more about them and discover how you can help them. They will be more willing to overcome their objections knowing that they have a person with whom to connect who can educate and inform them of their options and opportunities. Provide that personal touch.

## Recap

• When it comes to bringing in the business, conduct presentations is the best practice. Demonstrate the products in your homes, including the features, benefits and warranties—and do so in less obvious organizations.

• Establish an online presence that allows you to virtually share the value of your homes with others who aren't able to be reached in-person.

• Leverage the people you come in contact with. Get other people talking about the features and benefits of your products and services. Garner the interest and gain the referrals by networking, building your database, and making calls to ensure you are fully connecting with the people you've met.

## Crucial Questions

- "Am I finding ways to responsibly achieve my goals?"
- "What are new and unexpected places where I can present?
- "Do I have a Web presence for my presentations?"
- "Are my presentations affecting and influential?
- "Do they inform and educate?"
- "Am I leveraging relationships to support my goals?
- "Am I building my database?"
- "Am I networking adequately and making new contacts?"

# BEING A MASTER COMMUNICATOR

*"Success is fulfilling the needs, wants, hurts, and desires of another."*
— Dr. Robert Schuller

## Your Greeting

Being a master communicator begins with your very first interaction with a customer. Smile, look your customers in the eyes and extend your hand as you welcome them to your builder's homes. For example, you can say, *"Hi. Welcome to XYZ Homes. My name is Christine Hamilton. And you are?"*

First, acknowledge their arrival and your appreciation for their visit. State your builder or company name. This is more important than saying the community marketing name. Next, tell them your first and last name, not just your first name. Giving your last name in addition to your first name creates an impression of transparency and professionalism. When you give your full name, you can expect your customer to respond in kind and provide you with their full name as well. Finally, ask your first question, *"And you are?"* How you greet customers establishes the foundation for how your relationship will develop.

Once they give you their name, immediately write it down on a guest registration card. Write it down yourself because the customers will note your immediate interest in them. When you ask someone's name and immediately write it down, you are expressing that it them through the new home buying process.

34

You then ask, *"What brings you to look at new home sales today?"* You want to find out what got your new customer to this point of looking for a new home. This will open you up to finding out more about what your customer wants. A great segway question is, *"Do you have an idea of what size home and what price range you are looking for?"* This is where you'll begin to explore the customer's criteria.

## Ask to Truly Understand

As a new home salesperson, the smartest thing you can say or do is to ask questions! Asking questions is a fundamental part of establishing a rapport with customers and building their trust. On a basic level you can ask open-ended questions such as *"What made you decide to build on your own lot?"* to prompt the customers to share with you some of the features they're looking for in a home. But asking questions also allows you to tap into what is motivating a buyer and to magnify individual issues or interests—to build a responsible sense of urgency with regard to a customer's needs and wants.

When it comes to what customers want, it is up to the new home salesperson to help them prioritize their criteria. Customers aren't always clear themselves on what they want, which means you have to recognize that a customer's immediate responses should not necessarily be taken at face value. It's up to you to uncover which home best meets the customer's needs, wants, hurts and desires.

Being a successful new home salesperson in part requires uncovering all sides to a customer's situation. The hurts or the problems customers suffer are just as important as their practical needs or their vision of a dream home. Often, the surface answers only uncover the obvious, not delving deep enough into some of the more substantial reasons behind a customer's pursuit. Listen well to both what the customer is telling you and for what the customer is not telling you.

By asking questions that seek to illuminate gaps and draw out a customer's real reasons for looking for a new home. You set the stage for your presentation such that your customers will be infinitely more receptive to what you have to say. In doing so, they will recognize that you understand where they are coming from.

Asking questions allows you to tailor your presentation and model demonstration as a solution to your customer's needs. You gain the necessary knowledge to demonstrate the value and quality of your homes in the way in which the customer needs to hear it; to sell your homes in the way the customer needs to be sold. You never know when, or if, you will have a second chance with a customer. Odds are you won't have a second chance. It is imperative you not let the opportunity pass you by. So get real good at the art of asking.

## Dare to Dig

When it comes to asking customers questions, many new home salespeople think, *"I don't want to seem pushy"* or *"I don't want to pry"* because, although some people are looking at homes as leisure retreats, most people are searching for a home for a particular personal reason. Those reasons can manifest themselves on many levels, whether dissatisfaction with a current living situation or relationship troubles. It's not always easy for people to share what is difficult, share what is uncomfortable or unpleasant, or what doesn't look good in their lives.

As a front-line salesperson, get real with people real fast. Ask probing questions to create the space for your customers to feel comfortable opening up to you and sharing what's really going on in their lives that's motivating them to move now. When you dare to ask, they dare to share.

To ease into the discovery phase with the customer most empathetically, use Situation, Problem, Implication and Needs-Based Solution questions, also known as SPIN selling. Your ability to apply SPIN selling within your customers' experiences will not only differentiate you from other new home salespeople, but will ultimately contribute to a higher closing ratio. When you have the courage to ask, they have the courage to share. When you care enough to ask, they'll feel comfortable sharing.

*Situation Questions*

Within the realm of situation questions, it is important to work from macro to micro, from the big picture to the small picture. One of the things you want to know right up front is whether or not they searched online prior to coming in. The beginning point of most homebuyer searches commences on www-the World Wide Web. When going online, typical search words would be new homes, city and state. Most people, when considering purchasing or custom building a new home, choose the location first. They usually know which city or cities they are considering. a customer is considering any other places: *"Have you definitely decided on this city?"* or *"How did you decide on this location?"*

If you ask people about the location and you get an affirmative answer, then that part of their decision-making process is already done. Working from the location vantage point, you progress to the community. Ask customers, *"What prompted you to consider our community?"* and whether or not they conducted online searches prior to visiting your community. Right up front you'll uncover what your customer is already sold on and what he or she needs to learn more about.

After you get a feel for the customer's perception of community and location, progress to the product. Ask the customer—and this is a great way to knock out the option of a resale property—*"How important is it for you to have your home your way?"* If it is important to a customer to make his or her own selections, you know he or she is going to buy a new home. From there you can ask a customer, *"What is your timeline?"* And then take your question one step further by asking, *"What is your timeline based on?"* Sometimes a customer is still saving for a down payment, or has a home to sell first, or is expecting a baby, or is going through a divorce.

Any number of things can affect a timeline. But, no matter the timeline with which customers reply, it is important that you dig deeper to uncover what objection or concern or problem you may need to help them solve in order to move that timeline up to TODAY. Asking a customer questions about his or her timeline is a guaranteed moneymaker so long as you take the information you're given and use it to help the customer solve a problem.

Another important area of questioning in assessing a customer's situation is an individual's finances. Sample questions include, *"Have you talked to anyone yet about financing?"* and *"What amount have you been told you qualify for?"* or *"What type of loan are you considering?"* And, if you really want to impress a customer, *"What payment range do you comfortably want to stay within?"*—a question that signifies to a customer that you aren't going to push them beyond what they can afford. Once a customer shares with you the amount, you want to further the conversation by inquiring as to how he or she reached that number. You'll also need to ask, *"How much do you have saved for the down payment and closing costs?"*

The latter is important because the money doesn't have to be burning a hole in a customer's pocket that day if the house is yet to be built. The goal is to assess where a customer lies in terms of immediate interest and ability.

Situation questions allow for that initial assessment, and enable you to adjust the course of your conversation accordingly. You want to ask as many questions as you can right at the beginning. Before you fully present the community or share extensive information about the area or your builder, find out first where the customer is coming from. Sometimes they don't always know exactly what they want or what you have that they may like nor what they will accept as an alternative solution.

\*\*\*\*

*When I bought my very first brand new car, I was working in new home sales and had an old Volkswagen Jetta GLI with 187,000 miles on it. I loved my car and had previously worked selling Volkswagens, so I was very loyal to that product and had my heart set on a brand new Volkswagen Jetta GLX. Not only was I sure about what I wanted, I was sure that I had to have a red car with a tan interior, and that I absolutely did not want another car with black interior—I lived in a hot, dusty climate that absorbed heat and made every particle of dust or dirt visible.*

*I took my list of requirements to the dealership and learned that Volkswagen did not even offer that color combination. I went so far as to call the manufacturer and see if I could have it done custom, but that was not a possibility either. Feeling frustrated, I recalled another little car I had seen on the lot the day I went to the dealership—a pearl-colored Audi with black interior—and I fell in love. I ended up purchasing that pearl-colored Audi with the black interior which I had sworn I would never have again.*

*The point of this story is to illuminate that customers don't always know what they want. I thought I wanted a red Jetta GLI with tan interior. But instead, I ended up purchasing a nicer car with pretty color combination in a small four door German car with all the amenities. It was in fact, better than what I had originally envisioned for myself.*

****

You cannot always take what the customer initially says at face value. You've got to understand the underlying problems of the situation and the ensuing implications to be able to suggest an appropriate home solution. This is why you dig deeper into their reasons for moving and what they hope to achieve.

## Problem Questions

Problem questions take you to the next level in terms of understanding your customers. They often reveal what issues a customer is experiencing right then and there. The key problem question to ask is, *"Why have you decided to move?"* or, more specifically, *"Why are you considering purchasing or building a new home?"* or *"Why are you downsizing/upsizing?"* The act of downsizing or upsizing can be an immediate indicator of the type of problem(s) a customer is having. Someone may decide to downsize because utility bills are too high, or the mortgage is too expensive, or the amount of space is no longer needed, or because they want something more maintenance free, or because of health-related issues. Someone may decide to upsize because room is needed for a new baby, a blended family or because aging parents are moving in.

If you get your customer complaining—and this may seem contrary—but if you get your customer complaining, you're doing a good job. You want your customer to reveal his or her current dissatisfaction. Ask customers for details about the areas in which they live—the neighborhood and overall community, and the schools, shopping centers, parks, etc. nearby. That is what they don't like about where they live now and the home they live in.

Another very critical question to ask is the age of the home. Very few new home salespeople ask this question, but the answer is vital to gaining the information you need to know what you should present. If they live in any home that's 10 years old or more, it is likely to have features more antiquated heating and air conditioning or plumbing systems compared to the efficiency and effectiveness of today's new homes. This lets you know that you may need to talk about the comfort and convenience of owning a new energy-efficient home.

Within your problem questions you should also address the competition. If your customer is intent on buying a new home, chances are he or she is considering other builders. You need to find out exactly what locations, communities and homes your customers are exploring so that you can knock out the competition sooner rather than later.

Gracefully and professionally find out if your customer is considering any other homes seriously. Be sure you are well versed in what features and amenities the competition has to offer—what quality and value competitors profess in relation to your community's. Ask customers leading questions such as *"Are you seriously considering purchasing it?"* and *"Why haven't you purchased the home?"* or *"What was lacking?"*

Lastly, incorporate contingency inquiries into your problem questions. Beyond the age of a home, find out how long the customer has lived there or how long the client has owned the property. Find out when the customer bought it, what they paid for it, and how much they still owe on the property. Calculate how much the customer will net from the sale of the home. At this juncture, also don't be afraid to dig deeper by asking such questions as, *"Do you plan to sell in order to buy?"* or *"Have you considered renting it instead of selling?"* If their home is already on the market, ask, *"How competitively is it priced?"* Later in the conversation, you may go so far as to ask, *"If needed, are you willing to lower your price in order to get it sold in today's marketplace?"* Every problem question you ask is a lead in to the tailored solution you are about to present.

*Implication Questions*

Implication questions guide customers to consider the prices that they paying on a mental, emotional, financial and relationship level. Their answers also imply the consequences of not moving forward to a resolution.

As you dig into some of the problems that customers may be experiencing with regard to their current living situation, keep in mind that problems aren't always associated entirely with the house itself but may be more personal in nature. Gently ask about a customer's experience or circumstances. Reach inside his or her head and heart and empower yourself to best serve your customer with the information you unveil.

Some questions may focus on the personal life of a customer, such as *"How is that going?"* in response to a divorce-driven move, but the majority of implication questions will most likely center on the products you have to offer in your home. For example, if your customer's current home has a basement, you may ask *"Does your basement ever flood?" How do you get the water out?" "Are there any mold and mildew problems?" "Has that affected the health of you family yet or managed any of your belongings?"* Ask the customer what he or she does about a particular issue—especially if your homes propose a solution that you can then speak to. Ask about energy efficiency, hot and cold water features, vinyl- versus aluminum-clad windows.

There are countless implications stemming from household features that may be costing customers more money per month than they are willing or able to spend. Digging deep and asking implication questions allows you to approach customer issues more tactfully. Rather than pitching to a customer a generic perspective on how your homes can save more money, you can say, *"I wonder how much that is costing you?"* That type of rhetorical question causes the customer to reflect on what it's costing them and magnify the urgency of their need to take positive action now. They are also a lead in to present the features and benefits of your homes and community as the solution that will improve their life.

\*\*\*\*

*Early in my sales career I lost a sale to a competitor because I did not thoroughly know the features and benefits of the product I was selling. I was Facsimile Representative working for a Canon distributor. The company provided one week of training. But after only one week, I did not fully understand all of the features of the L770, our bestselling plain paper fax machine. Specifically, I knew nothing about delayed transmission, a feature that gives the end user the ability to delay the transmission of faxes until after business hours when phone rates are significantly lower. After I had lost the sale to a competitor, the customer phoned me and asked if our fax machine offered delayed transmission. I looked into it and called the customer back to let him know that yes, it did indeed. But at that point, the deal was done. He had already purchased a lower priced fax machine from my competitor. Unfortunately, the majority of the faxes that they sent were to long distant numbers. Had I understood all of the features of our machine, I may have uncovered the fact that they were spending a lot of money in long distance charges. I could have provided them a more suitable solution which would have saved them a significant amount of money in long distant charges and thereby justified our higher price. In the end, this resulted in a lose-lose-lose situation. The customer lost the opportunity to purchase a fax machine better suited to their needs and save money. I lost a sale and a potential commission. And, my company lost potential revenue. Therefore, it is very important for companies to invest the time and money in product knowledge training.*

*Likewise, proactive companies provide training in their competitor's products. By knowing and understanding the competition, well-informed sales representatives better differentiate their company's products from their competitor's. You have got to know about the competition before you can successfully sell against them.*

*From then on out I did my homework on any product I sold, including new homes, so that I would understand the features and benefits that made it distinct in quality. Furthermore, I would generate a list of the dozen or so best features of my product and some sample questions I would want to know the answers to. This gave me a more complete picture of the benefits of my product so that I could more readily solve any problem a customer had.*

****

By not only knowing what questions to ask yourself but anticipating what types of questions your customers may ask, you can cater to the different personality types of your customers. Some customers may be feeling-type people for whom your implication questions appeal to emotional senses: *"How do you feel about that?"* For other customers who are calculating by nature, you can tailor your implication question to appeal to their analytical sensibilities. For example, you may ask a customer how much money he or she is spending monthly and yearly on a rental. *"I wonder how much rent that is per year?"* By doing so, you guide the customer to consider the benefits and savings that result from purchasing one of your homes—effectively making better investment of their money.

Implication questions essentially highlight the costs of the customer staying where he or she is currently versus the benefits of making a change: *"What is it costing you?"* or *"How is it affecting your budget?"* and *"What would you do with the money otherwise?"* Notice that you don't need to answer the question yourself or state the obvious. Just plant the seed by asking a question. This is another example of the art of guiding the customers thought process.

As you ask the right implication questions, you will effectively magnify the customer's sense of urgency. When you ask these questions, you guide customers' thinking in such a way that they are able to vocalize and share with you the circumstances surrounding their new home search. By the time you meet a customer, he or she has already come to you with a desire to buy, or at least to learn more. The urgency is embedded. It is your job to magnify it; to bring to the surface the myriad reasons the customer may want or need to move. There is always a reason to buy and always a reason to do it right here, now, today. It is your job, your responsibility, to find what that reason is for your customer.

*Need-based Solutions*

After you've used your questions to assess the situation, identify the problems, and uncover the implications, the final step is to ask the questions that gauge the customer's receptivity towards a need-based solution. You may ask, *"If you found the right house today, would you buy it?"* or *"When you find the right house, when do you plan on buying it?"* Recall the problems, concerns and objections the customer voiced that may prevent him or her from moving forward today and ask, *"If I showed you a way to purchase today, would you be open to that?"* Provide customers with solution options by asking them questions that open them to the possibilities. Whatever a customer's personal reason— if the down payment isn't completely saved, or if the divorce isn't final, or if the current home isn't yet sold—remind the customer that escrow won't be closed today. One of the many perks of a new home is that it takes time to build. Customers don't have to have all their ducks in a row that same day. They just have to have enough earnest money for the deposit.

*"If I showed you a way, would you buy today?"* Be the response to their situation, the resolution to their problems, and the clarity to their implications. Be the solution to their needs.

## Power of Listening

As a new home salesperson, the greatest power you possess is the willingness and ability to listen to what customers have to say. As you regularly interact with diverse customers approaching you for a range of reasons, both apparent and hidden, your first and foremost way of helping them is to listen intently to what they say and how they express themselves. It is only by listening that you can then ask the questions that a customer needs to answer, such that they can hear aloud their own responses.

### The Possibilities

A critical part of listening to your customers is first recognizing that every customer is an opportunity—that a wide range of possibilities unfolds whenever a customer walks into your sales center. The only way you can help a customer buy a home, and help yourself achieve your sales goals, is to know that whether or not a customer can or will buy at that moment, that customer will now be an ambassador of your service and the experience you delivered.

Being a master communicator is about recognizing your power and the effect you have or can have on your customers. Always remember to consciously ask questions that open up the possibilities.

## Recap

• Being a master communicator requires perfecting the art of asking. This is completely centered upon the mindset that you can solve a customer's problem and show him or her how to move forward today. Empower yourself to that end. Artfully ask the questions that will enable you to help the customers who seek you out.

• Find out what your customer's perspective is before moving on to the presentation of your builder, community and homes.

## Crucial Questions

• *"Hi. Welcome to XYZ Homes. My name is Christine Hamilton. And you are?"*
• *"What brings you to look at new home sales today?"*
• *"Do you have an idea of what size home and what price range you are looking for?"*
• *"Did you search online prior to coming in?"*
• *"How did you decide on this location?"*
• *"What prompted you to consider our community?"*
• *"How important is it for you to have your home your way?"*
• *"Why have you decided to move? Why are you considering purchasing or building a new home?"*
• *"What is your timeline? What is it based on?"*
• *"Are you seriously considering any other communities or homes? What was lacking that you didn't purchase the home yet?"*
• *"Do you plan to sell/rent in order to buy?"*
• *"Are you willing to lower your price in order to get it sold in today's marketplace?"*
• *"How's it going? How do you feel about that?"*
• *"How much are you paying per month in rent?"*
• *"I wonder how much that comes to per year?"*
• *"What is it costing you? How is it affecting your budget? What would you do with the money otherwise?"*
• *"If you found the right house today, would you buy it?"*
• *"If I showed you a way to purchase today, would you be open to that?"*

# MASTERING PERSONALITY SELLING

*"I have a dream that my four little children will one day live in a nation where they will not be judged by the color of their skin, but by the content of their character."*

— Martin Luther King, Jr.


## Building Relationships

When it comes to the new home sales scenario, the idea that "opposites attract" doesn't hold up. People tend to buy from people they like. And, people tend to like those who are like themselves. Therefore, adjusting your behavior, oftentimes, is an integral part of connecting with another individual on their level. To be an effective Sales PROfessional you have to sell customers the way they like to be sold, not necessarily the way you are used to selling or how you like to be sold to. Sell customers in the ways *they* need and want to be sold. Help customers buy the way they need and want to buy.

Figuring out how a customer needs and wants to be buy requires determining an individual's character type. Determining someone's character type begins during your initial greeting with a simple handshake. As a practice that should be integral to all your customer interactions, handshakes are an instantaneous way gauge character. Take a customer's hand in your own and look him or her in the eye and say, *"Hi, welcome to XYZ community. My name is… and you are?"* Be in that moment and be observant.

Feel the way in which the customer shakes your hand. Listen to the way they respond to your question. Pay close attention to their word choices and the way in which they say them. Observe their body language. All of these factors will clue you into his or her character type. Once you figure out the character type, you will have a guide for all customer interactions thereafter as you work to close the deal.

## Four Character Types: CAPS

Overall, there are four character types that describe and define each individual person and serve as the foundation for interpersonal engagement: Controller, Analyst, Promoter, Supporter (CAPS). Each person possesses varying degrees of the characteristics that comprise the different quadrants. Undoubtedly, though, most people have a primary personality type, followed by a secondary one. These two types are defined by certain qualities being more pronounced than others. When it comes to your customers, you want to ascertain what each person's primary and secondary quadrants are. It's also imperative that you know which personality quadrants(s) you are and which you struggle with the most. This will enable you to adjust your behavior to more closely mirror that of your customer and maximize your ability to connect with them on their level.

### The Controller

Controllers are doers. You'll be able to tell this from the first handshake. The controller isn't shy about shaking hands. You'll receive a firm grip that seeks to establish dominance right from the beginning. That firm grip will also signify a no-nonsense approach. The controller is a business-first type of person, focused on getting things done, not on establishing a friendship. If you want to relate to the controller on the controller's level, you've got to get down to business first. The personal part of the relationship will be secondary.

Because controllers are results-oriented people, they are the most interested in the bottom line. Though they are outgoing, extroverted individuals, they are not necessarily going to exhibit excitement. They are relatively unemotional individuals who tend to be assertive and strong-willed, often intimidating and especially impatient. For controllers, impatience, albeit contrary to popular opinion, is a point of pride because it's what inherently makes them action-oriented. It is the quality they rely on most to get things done. Controllers are independent, high achievers and immensely efficient. They also tend to be decisive and high-risk takers, unafraid to make buying decisions immediately.

When it comes to buying a home, one thing that is critical to remember about controllers is that they tend to be headstrong and confident. It is based on an inherent need to be right—or at least thing think they are right things. Without insult or judgment this is another quality that makes them confident and decisive as homebuyers.

## Adjusting to the Controller

Because the controller will want to control the direction of the interaction, they will tend to ask very pointed and direct questions about the community, prices, amenities and financing. Regardless of the subject, you had better give them a direct answer to a direct question. You had better know your stuff. If you don't know the answer to something, attempt to get an answer immediately. the controller expects and respects responsiveness.

When it comes to the demonstration of your model—because the controller is so strong and domineering—you want to show the power and prestige of the home. For example, if your home has a nice, dark, stately exterior elevation, speak to how such an exterior design makes a statement and is powerful-looking. Appeal to the controller's sense of power and prestige.

Inside the home, the controller will tend to like the view from the entry, the office and the living rooms. Be sure to highlight any awe-inspiring views that give a sense of grandeur. As a Sales PROfessional for a new home builder, it's important to consider that controllers often like to customize their homes from the ground up. They won't always want to settle for a home that is complete, demanding instead to make their own selections regarding floors, countertops and paint colors. They want to have it *their* way. Building a one-of-a-kind home is often a very important factor for the controller.

When it comes to your discussions with the controller about the home, you should remain to-the-point. They are direct, bottom-line people. They are interested only in necessary information and not extraneous details. You don't have to schmooze with a controller because the controller isn't going to be sold based on a friendly relationship. He or she is going to make the decision to buy based on the information he or she thinks is pertinent.

Controllers will ask direct questions. In responding to their questions, it's important to provide direct answers. Be straightforward and forthright. But also take the opportunity to ask questions after you've answered them. Be careful not to enter into a power play with the controller.

It's important to strike a balance that positions the controller in an dominant role while simultaneously enabling you to stand just as tall and be just as self-assured in what it is you have to offer. Controllers will respect your confidence, just as they prize their own!

Another incredibly important factor in identifying and connecting with a controller is your level of responsiveness. This means answering their questions in a timely manner and scheduling appointments right away. Get answers to their questions on the spot. If you don't know an answer to a question, admit it—never wing it. Pursue the answer immediately so all matters are accomplished right away. Controllers respect your competence. Keep the sales experience moving forward. You will increase your close ratio with controllers. The more prompt service you extend in assisting them accomplish their task of finding, purchasing and closing on their new home, the more controller prospects you will convert to buyers.

When it comes to the close, the controller is not afraid to buy on the first day. Seize on that and ask the question directly: *"Do you want to buy it?"* They will not be offended; just be direct. As you seek to seal the deal, one measure that is very effective with controllers is the take-away close. If you ask a controller whether he or she is interested in buying a home and you receive noncommittal answer, provide a little push: *"Well, if you don't buy it someone else will."* Let that controller know that somebody else is interested and that it only takes one lucky buyer. The controller never wants to lose control. The fear of losing control and the possibility of having to settle for second best as an alternative choice are great motivators for them.

Once the decision has been made to buy, approach the purchase agreement in an efficient, business-oriented way. Cut to the chase and only go over the important details, spending no more than 45 minutes to complete the paperwork. In most instances, the controller will want to be in-and-out of the office. Cater to his or her individual sense of urgency—it will magnify your opportunity for success with the controller each and every time.

*The Analyst*

Analysts are thinkers. They are conscientious, cerebral people. The analyst's handshake will most likely be curt and fairly formal, to the point but not dominating. Similar to the controller, the analyst will establish a business-first relationship with you, but it will also be an intellectual connection. Though very intelligent, their approach will be reserved as opposed to assertive. They tend to keep quiet about their thoughts as they process what you have to say.

As independent people, analysts tend to be calculating and relatively unemotional with regard to their decision-making. They are orderly and organized, and tend to be perfectionists. A true mark of the analyst's personality is being detail-oriented. As professionals, they likely work with facts and figures which indicate that those types of details will greatly influence their home buying decision. Being driven by the details also means that the analyst is persistent and doesn't give up easily. They don't allow themselves to be distracted and they are incredibly thorough, which means their decision to buy may be a slow one.

It is important to note that thoroughness does not indicate an inability to make a decision. Rather, it means the analyst will only make a decision with what he or she considers sufficient information. Unlike the controller who thinks he or she is right, the analyst has an inherent need to *not* be wrong. For people who pride themselves on being able to understand quantitative information and come to an informed conclusion, being wrong is one of the worst things that can happen for them. In working with this group as a salesperson, one of your primary responsibilities is to honor he analysts' need for information and assist them in their analysis.

Adjusting to the Analyst

When it comes to demonstrating your homes, a great way to appeal to the analyst is to show the logic and functionality behind the floor plans. Also take every opportunity to show analysts the organizational properties of the home, whether it's a linen closet in each bathroom or a built-in desk in the office. Show them features that relate the orderly and exacting aspects of their personalities to the home.

Knowing too that the analyst is attracted to numbers, talk to analyst customers about price per square foot. That will be a value that really resonates with them. The analyst will also appreciate a comparison of energy efficiency. They will want to see if you can show their exact savings per month and your ability to do so will be a huge selling point. Another comparison to provide them with is the percentages for the homes that sell in your community. For example, if Plan One accounts for 25 percent of your sales, Plan 2 for 40 percent, and Plans 3 and 4 account for the other 35 percent, that's an immediate indicator of your most popular plan. Analysts will recognize that Plan 2 translates to being better on resale value. More importantly, analysts will compare your homes. Make sure you know the competition well. The analysts will do their homework.

They are a prime customer group to share your competition book with because they will appreciate the time, energy, and thought you put into analyzing the features and benefits while forming an objective comparison of your homes and community. Analysts like to see the comparative market analysis which can be proof of value of what they're considering purchasing from you.

When interacting with the analyst slow down your presentation. If you typically conduct a more exciting, upbeat presentation, temper the tempo so as not to overwhelm or over-stimulate the analyst. Allow for moments of silence. Give them the opportunity to think and process what you're presenting. The more they absorb the information you share, the more they'll be sold and sell themselves on the home. Because analysts are very precise individuals, it's important that you remember to be exacting in how you conduct your presentation, and practice patience with them as well. You need to be detail-oriented and thorough right along with them—never wing it. Know your stuff.

An analyst will not stand to be deceived in any way, and chances are, because they are so analytical, they will catch any and all of your inconsistencies. Be overly prepared when it comes to knowing your facts, figures and information. Try your best not to make mistakes because these cerebral people will notice. The way you relate to them should be straightforward and serious; they will not often respond to schmoozing or humor. Remember, the point is to better connect with the customer, which means approaching them in ways that feel comfortable to them. Catering to their exactness and thoroughness builds their trust in you.

In terms of closing, the analyst is less likely to move forward on the first visit to your community—but that doesn't mean he or she won't. An important consideration for the analyst will likely know exactly how he or she is going to finance the home. If you are well versed in discussing financing options, it will give you an advantage in closing the analyst sooner because he or she will feel comfortable in your knowledge and expertise. However, only discuss financing with the analyst if you can do so competently and in accurate detail—for example, be able to adjust interest pro-rations and tax pro-rations depending on what month or day the customer's new home will close. If your analyst customer has already spoken with a lender, you can be sure that he or she is going to compare your numbers to the information received before.

Beyond the financial, ask analysts what else they need to help them decide: *"What other information do you need to formulate a decision?"* Also remember to ask, *"Are there any other homes you're considering seriously?"* to get a sense of their comparison. Appeal to their personality type by using a comparative close in which you show a T-bar and side-by-side comparison of any other homes they may be considering. As you provide them with all the competitive information and analysis of options, pose a logical question. Ask them if it makes sense to move forward with your home, or if they think that your home is better quality and a better value.

Similar to the controller, you don't want to immediately give incentives with the analyst. The analyst will perceive that as the starting point for negotiation. So they will typically need to think it over one day and try and get more out of you the next. Keep the conversation focused on facts and figures. Ask the analyst, *"Is this a home that you indeed want to own?"* and if the answer is *"Yes,"* move forward. If your analyst customer does not want to close right away, diligently follow up and be sure to provide even more relevant information. One of the greatest services you provide an analyst is competent information—give analysts what they need to make decisions in their way. Remember also that the art of asking questions is to skillfully use questions to help guide a customer's thinking.

When it comes time to do the purchase agreement, allow as much time to do the paperwork as necessary. Be as thorough as needed for the analyst, carefully going over the purchase agreement, disclosures, reports, CC&Rs, homeowner's association documents and the like. As part of their independence, analysts may want to take it and read it themselves, but you need to also be fully prepared to discuss every item in your disclosures and white reports. You can safely assume the analyst will have questions, so be prepared to answer. Guide them through every step of the process and you will guide yourself to the result you want.

## *The Promoter*

Promoters are talkers. They are happiest communicating and engaging with others. Oftentimes, when a promoter comes to your sales center, he or she will give you an excited, vigorous handshake. You will feel a lot of energy come off of that individual, and that's how you can tell a promoter from the other personality types right from the beginning.

Promoters are influential, popular people. They tend to be relationship-first, not business-first. It's important for them to make a friendly connection with you because they're looking to have fun through the home-buying experience. It is especially true for this group that home buying is an *experience* and not a *process*. They wear their emotions right on their sleeve, so you'll always know what's going on with them and how they're feeling through the experience. The promoter is a true people-person. Engaging, enthusiastic, and fun, the promoter will seek to build a strong connection with you.

Promoters are often spontaneous, so you don't necessarily need to schedule with them ahead of time. They are not detail-oriented. They are multi-taskers, which may seem like a lack of focus. They prefer to be in the moment and seek out stimulating experiences and are easily distracted. They are also ambitious and assertive. Promoters enjoy the limelight, which means they will want and expect your attention. When it comes to buying, promoters are quick to decide. Their need for excitement is part of what drives them to make a decision.

## Adjusting to the Promoter

One of the promoter's favorite areas of the home is where the entertainment happens. If your homes have a great room or a family room that opens up to the kitchen, the promoter will gravitate toward this space because the promoter likes to entertain. Promoters also love the bedrooms and bathrooms, particularly the more luxurious features of each. Outdoor living spaces are incredibly important as an additional area to engage with people. They are big on quality lifestyles— promoters will be drawn to amenities within your community such as a clubhouse, pool or spa where they can socialize with others. They'll also be interested in your community's proximity to arts, entertainment, shopping, nightlife, or other public places that play to the promoter's social life.

As you demonstrate the home to a promoter, make a point to use his or her name. Promoters like to hear their name because it makes them feel important and loved. It's important that you reinforce that friendship-based relationship with them by appealing to them directly as individuals. Because promoters are keen on close relationships, it is important that you not adversely affect the rapport you build. Similar to the controller, you do not want to disagree with the promoter for the most part. The promoter wants to be treated specially, which means catering to an individual's feelings and interests. In your demonstration, take every opportunity to emphasize how the home and community are special. Get them excited about owning the home by asking leading questions: *"Wouldn't it be exciting if... ?"* or *"Can you imagine... ?"* Again, play to the importance of social relationships in their lives. *"What do you think your friends are going to say when you show them your new home?"* The promoter cares about what other people think, so posing questions that bring in that influence is a great way to magnify urgency.

If you excite the promoter, he or she will have no problem making a decision that day. Ask them if they are excited about purchasing this home. You can simply assume the sale.

When you do get the go-ahead, simplify the purchase agreement. The promoter will most likely not feel a need to read the document and will be immediately ready to sign. Be sure to let them know any important details so you can set the expectations for what they need to do, but otherwise don't bore them with details. Keep the things moving and keep it fun. If you drag it out, the promoter may start to rethink things. Make it enjoyable because the promoter is the primary personality type that will promote you, your company and your homes.

Remember, promoters are influential and popular people as well as expert communicators. Don't be afraid to ask for referrals because the promoter can and will bring you more business. Once the promoter has purchased one of your homes, your community will be touted as the best there is in the new home arena. Connect promoters to their dream homes and they'll connect you to success.

If for some reason you can't close the promoter that first day, follow up with an engaging telephone call and shoot him or her an email full of colorful photos of the home. These experiences will affirm your friendship and help the promoter build that beautiful vision of the new home in this or her own mind.

*The Supporter*

Supporters are listeners. When a supporter greets you in your sales center, he or she will tend to have a soft and gentle handshake, maybe even a little flimsy. Likewise, loosen your grip in return. Supporters are extremely friendly people, but in a quiet way. They are very caring, often emphasizing how others feel over how they feel. They're sensitive to what is going on around them—one of the supporter's greatest qualities is empathy, which makes them very attuned to others. Supporters are peacekeepers and as such tend to be agreeable. They're very willing and dependable, and will usually do what is asked of them. They are very cooperative and compliant and, similar to promoters, also very emotional.

Because supporters are not very assertive people, they can be difficult to read. Like the analyst, they are somewhat reserved. For them, a kind relationship is the absolute most important thing. Business is the lowest priority on their list. What they need to feel the most is trust. You need to step into a space with them where you're working on building a caring relationship. As you work with the supporter, be aware that he or she may be slow to make decisions, and may even have a change of mind. But more often than not, the supporter will involve or defer decisions to others. Position yourself to be of service and support them in making a decision. They may also defer to you to help them make a decision or allow you to make it for them.

When it comes to buying a home, the supporter's driving force is often the need for approval from other people and to please others. Supporters take everyone in their family into considerations and try to meet the needs of everyone who will be living in and visiting the home. Because they place so much emphasis on others, safety, security and family are incredibly important to supporters. As you engage them in the home-buying process, seek to understand and support their quest to please other people. That's how you will win the supporter's heart and trust.

Adjust to the Supporter

Service should be a central concern for you in working with supporters. Supporters will recognize the efforts you make to serve their needs and interests, because that is what they do in their own relationships. They appreciate any act of kindness or generosity. Such acts make them feel more comfortable in your hands and more capable in their decision-making.

Personal relationships are a huge priority for the supporter, so in selling to the supporter you also have to sell to the people they surround themselves with. They care about the people in their lives, especially family and friends—so part of your demonstration has to touch on how the home and community will meet the needs of those they care about.

As extremely family-oriented people, supporters are drawn to the hearth and areas like the kitchen, dining and family rooms—especially if they are open to each other. If your homes offer or include a fireplace, show it to supporters as a focal point around which they can envision the coziness and delight of a family gathered around the hearth together. Dining rooms are a great point of focus because supporters like knowing that everyone can be seated at the same table, having dinner together. A courtyard or outdoor area will also attract their attention as more family space, as will features like hardwood floors, which impart a sense of warmth to the home. If your homes offer a casita or have secondary bathrooms to accommodate guests or larger families, it can tip the supporter's desire to buy in your favor. Supporters like knowing that their home will be a place for people to come and stay. Along with that, they also appreciate a sense of community, and a community that prizes safety and security.

More so than any other personality type, the supporter needs to feel the presence of your company's customer care department. Supporters want to know that your company is going to be there for them before, during and after the sale. As a Sales PROfessional, you need to be a ready resource for the supporter, providing a lot of presale customer services and engaging with the supporter on a meaningful level. For example, if a supporter begins to talk about his or her family and you can see sensitive emotions emerging, step into that feeling. Ask supporters to show you pictures and show them pictures in return—any photos of your family you may have sitting on your desk. As you do so, share a story about those important to you. It will open supporters up and get them to tell you about their own family, which will be precisely those for whom they're looking to buy a house. If you connect with supporters on the heart level, you will gain their trust.

Similar to the analyst, be sure to be exceedingly patient with supporters. They will take more time to decide because they most likely have more than one person they're trying to please. Use a soft and comforting tonality when you converse with them to keep a level of calm, for the supporter may find the home-buying experience unnerving to a certain degree.

Supporters also appreciate opportunities to break bread with you, so to speak. If you're meeting with a supporter in your sales center and have the means to do so, offer coffee, tea or water and a little something to eat. As you tour them through your models, take a moment to sit with them on the furniture. Acts of hospitality will immediately put them at ease and help you build a bond. Supporters also appreciate gifts, so another nice gesture may be to offer a token, such as a company pen, when they leave or after they sign. Supporters appreciate even the smallest acts of kindness.

When it comes to helping the supporter commit to a course of action, inquire as to how he or she feels. A great question to ask is "*Do you feel like your family would be happiest in this home?*" If you receive a "*Yes,*" move forward with it immediately. Don't give the supporter time to change his or her mind. As you seek to close, don't apply pressure. Never use a takeaway close—the supporter will let the opportunity be taken from them simply because they wouldn't want to make waves or hurt anyone else's feelings.

Once the supporter has agreed to the purchase, reaffirm the decision. Reinforce the decision to buy and tell the supporter that he or she deserves it, and family members deserve it. Make the decision touch the supporter on a personal level. Help supporters see and feel that a home is right for them, doing so in a kind way. If you have established enough of a relationship with a supporter and you truly feel that the decision to buy is the right one—that you have done your work with this customer and are helping to make the best decision for the supporter's entire family— tenderly lead them through the process.

If the supporter seems stuck in fear, simply start going over the purchase agreement in a smooth manner. Because supporters are compliant people, they will usually follow right along. Help them feel comfortable in the decision to buy and you can be confident in the outcome you reach.

If you don't close the supporter right away, ensure your follow-ups are friendly and attentive. Take the opportunity to build the relationship further.

## Power and Value

You won't close 100 percent of the prospects in any given community. But, as you become better at identifying and conforming to the personality type of your customer, you will increase your close ratio to close 100 percent of the *possible* sales. That's the power and value behind mastering personality selling.

## Recap

• You can gain a good sense of a customer's personality type right from the initial handshake. When you meet a customer, ask yourself which CAPS a customer wears on his or her head during each and every greeting. Also be aware of which one(s) you wear. Be sure to modify your CAPS depending upon the type of person with whom you are interacting.

• Controllers are results-oriented doers and tend to be very assertive, relatively unemotional, and very decisive. They are the most commanding of all four personality types.

• Analysts tend to be calculating thinkers who are relatively unemotional. They are not assertive and are also slower to decide because of their thorough nature.

• Promoters are talkative socialites. They are also highly emotional, which means that they are impulsive buyers and spontaneous decision makers.

• Supporters are the most empathic of the four personalities. Like the analysts, they are not very assertive. They tend to be emotional but are relatively indecisive and will often defer important decisions to be made by others.

## Crucial Questions

• *"My name is..., and you are?"*

Controller
• *"Do you want to buy it?"*

Analyst
• *"What other information do you need to formulate a decision?"*
• *"Are there any other homes you're considering seriously?"*
• *"Is this a home that you indeed want to own?"*

Promoter
• *"Wouldn't it be exciting if...? Can you imagine...?"*
• *"What do you think your friends are going to say when you show them your new home?"*

Supporter
• *"Do you feel like your family would be happiest in this home?"*

# A PERFECT DEMONSTRATION

*"Seek first to understand, then to be understood."*
                                    – Dr. Stephen R. Covey

****

*I can recall a particular mid-week visit I made to a builder in a high-traffic area. Within an hour, four customer groups visited the builder's model complex—excellent traffic especially for the middle of the week. I noticed, though, that both salespeople and their assistant stayed camped out in the sales center the entire time answering customer questions, getting visitor surveys completed and instructing customers where to go and see the available home sites. I later asked the sales director, "What is their sales conversion ratio?" Her answer was one percent, which means that only one in 100 people who came through their sales center purchase a home. That's a ridiculously low number.*

*When I worked on the front line, I remember, on any given weekend day, grand openings with as many as 300 to 400 people in attendance. My sales center was a competitive floor, which meant that whoever wrote and closed the sale earned the entire commission.*

*Even on the busiest days, I would spend time in the models with customers, getting to know them, demonstrating the features, helping them select a home site, closing and completing purchase agreements. As a result, I typically was responsible for 63 to 75 percent of the sales in each of my communities. There's no better way to win over customers and close deals than to take them through the perfect demonstration.*

****

## Your Models Are Your Moneymakers

Homes don't sell themselves, you do. Think of your model homes as your moneymakers and work your moneymakers.

Strive for quality time spent with your customers as opposed to quantity of contacts. Consider the customer's perspective: visiting four or five builders in any given day and viewing 12 to 15 models. There are many similarities in the new home marketplace and the models begin to look alike after a while. It's hard to remember them all. Sometimes the customer will remember a particular home—for example, if it is exceptionally well merchandised or if the model is deconstructed to show the materials used—but more often than not, the customer remembers the service experience that you extended!

A true Sales PROfessional doesn't just spew out a list of features and benefits, but demonstrates them and gets the customer involved. Moreover, it is the key to appealing to each customer's distinct wants and needs, and to differentiating your homes from the competition.

In new home sales, the builder, purchasing department, and design team are incredibly deliberate about the products and components chosen to be included in your homes. Often, the difference in products from new home to new home truly is in the details. Consider the floor plans, material brands, features, warranties, energy efficiency and more— recognize the importance of each of these aspects and become well-versed in communicating their benefits as you seek to demonstrate the value of your homes. When you point out the included features in your homes, help your customers notice the differences in the details, you are helping them differentiate your builder and homes from everything else available.

****

*When I was considering returning to real estate as a sales manager after taking an extended family leave to raise my son, I decided to anonymously shop the salespeople I would be leading. At one community, I noticed a plastic panel in the garage that I didn't recognize. I asked one of the salespeople what it was. It was clear to me he didn't really know, as I couldn't even make sense of his answer. So, I asked another salesperson. This time I was told it was a plumbing manifold, but was given no further explanation.*

*As a "potential buyer" that spoke volumes to me. For customers who are coming in and considering purchasing a new home, such ill-informed answers may cause them to doubt the competence and credibility of the salespeople and the quality of the homes. Lack of sufficient product knowledge results in a loss of potential sales.*

****

## You Set the Context

On the front line, sales PROfessionals have the power to make a significant difference in the minds of customers by spending quality time with their customers versus going for quantity of contacts.

It is the salespeople who set the context for a wonderful customer-centric, service-oriented home buying experience, in large part by demonstrating homes while continuing to ask incisive, insightful questions. The way to grant your customers a wonderful model tour is to engage their senses, getting them to see and touch the home, and envision themselves making the move and living there.

## Before You Begin

Every morning before you open make sure your models are ready! Check that the exterior is clean and the front porch is free of bugs and cobwebs. Survey the landscaping to ensure plants are alive and green with no rubbish in the yard. The entryway of each home should be spotless. Make sure windows, mirrors and other glass or reflective surfaces are smudge-free. Ensure the floors are spotless. Straighten any furniture, including beds and pillows, so that everything looks untouched and perfect. Make sure the interior wall paint and baseboards are impeccable. Turn on every light and make sure all the bulbs are working.

It is important to note the power of scent—some companies make a practice of baking fresh cookies to provide the house with an enticing, comforting aroma. Sound is important too. Keep WD-40 on-hand so that your doors are oiled and remain squeak-free. It is your responsibility to ensure that your models are impeccably clean, that there are neither foul odors nor bothersome sounds. As you seek to enhance the customer experience, ensure that negative conditions don't detract from customers' first impressions of your homes. The bottom line is that it is your responsibility to walk your models bottom-to-top, end-to-end every morning and night to make sure they are ready for show time.

## Assume Permission

After you've thoroughly checked your models to ensure they're ready for customers, the first step in initiating a demonstration is to assume permission to accompany your customer into the model. After you've had an in-depth discovery conversation with the customer in the sales center, guide the customer into the first model.

Your lead-in can be, *"Let's go take a look at our model home."* Or, if the model you have available is different than the plan your customer is considering, simply adjust your invitation accordingly: *"Although the model home is different than the plan that I think you will like best, let's take a look at the model and I will show you how the plans are similar and point out some of our quality amenities."* Use your model to demonstrate the value of your homes, even when you don't currently have a model of what the customer seeks.

## Be Methodical

*Start with the Exterior*

A good model demonstration is relatively methodical. As you exit your sales center, begin at the exterior of the first home. As you exit your sales center, pause as far back as possible on the sidewalk in front of your first model, whether it's the only one you have or the first of several. Choose a place to stop where there is a comprehensive view. Begin to point out and describe the exterior design features. If you have multiple elevations within your community, describe and point out the stylistic differences of each.

Perhaps your community has a Spanish style, a Mediterranean style and an Italian style, or perhaps you have contemporary and traditional versions. Whatever the case, point out the different roof lines, window grid patterns, arches over doorways, decorative corbels, the front door, the porch, address numbers, gutters, downspouts and more. Take the time to help customers appreciate your builder's attention to detail and the home's aesthetic features and the quality of construction. A pleasing curb appeal strongly affects the receptiveness of a customer upon passing through the front door.

*Now Step Inside*

Once you have called attention to the details on the outside, step just inside the front door and pause in the entry. Allow the customer to get a solid, sweeping view of the inside of the home. Pause long enough for their first impression of the interior to sink in.

If you have a large model home, position your customers where their eyes can travel across interior spaces and rooms, and out to outdoor living areas. Chances are a larger home is an expensive home, so you must be sure to point out where the value is.

For example, in many East Coast homes, morning rooms are a commonly desired feature as they extend the kitchen and dining area. The inclusion of that option may not only be highly desirable but may also mean the addition of 100-150 square feet. Similarly, the option to finish a basement within a particular home could add hundreds of livable square feet at a price point that creates a tremendous value.

As you address these considerations and the model as a whole, especially be aware of how customers respond to the differences in floor plans and configurations. Many people have strong preferences with regard to where the master bedroom is located or how central living space is situated. Ask questions about those spatial preferences and be prepared to point out and discuss differences and options.

Guide your customers to experience each room of the house from different angles and be sure to acknowledge architectural details that they may find attractive or unique. Engage them in the model experience by asking questions that encourage them to thoughtfully consider the home for their intended use.

When looking at prospective homes, customers bring different needs and wants with regard to the form and function of each room. It is your job to uncover and address their desires. As you show each room, sprinkle your presentation with test questions such as *"What do you think?"* or *"How would you use/decorate this room?"* and *"How would your furniture fit in here?"* These test questions help show how you are doing and how well the customer likes the home so far. You may learn that you are on the right track or that you need to adjust.

<u>Family Room</u>

As you guide your customers into the living areas, encourage them to stand back, as if taking the perspective of a photographer, so they can take in the entire space. Invite them to sit on the furniture so they experience how enjoyable it would be to spend time in that room. Ask them questions: *"How would your furniture work in this room?"* or *"How would you decorate this living room?"* and *"What do you think about the coffered ceiling, windows, archways and crown molding featured in this home? Isn't it pretty?"*

Focus on the included features such as ceiling heights and counter space if there is open concept between the kitchen and great room. Draw attention to features such as recessed lighting, ceiling fan pre-wire, the fireplace and hearth, and rocker or toggle light switches. Never assume that customers will notice these details—help them appreciate the quality of construction and attention to detail.

## Kitchen

The kitchen is an interesting place and is a space where people often have very particular requirements. Be sure to slow people down within the kitchen. You can begin with a really basic but engaging question: *"Do you like to cook?"*

Note such features as whether cabinets are 36 or 42 inches in height and whether there is pretty molding above the cabinetry or if there is space above for decorative items or if they go to the ceiling. Call attention to shelves that are fully adjustable and soft-closing drawers. Point out the impressive size of the island and engage the customer by asking, *"How many barstools do you think you could fit around it?"* Be sure to point out appliance brands and their features and benefits.

Remember that you can make even the most standard features sound great. Even if your homes are built just like everyone else's, if you point out the included features and present them as quality products in your homes, then you are building value in the mind of the customer. Building strong associations between your home and an enhanced lifestyle could mean the difference in a customer's decision-making. Lead the customer to visualize and experience the home in terms of his or her own dream.

## Master Suite

For many homebuyers, the master suite is a huge draw. Similarly to walking into the front door, stop just inside the entry of the master suite and give the customer time to really view this intimate area. Point out the size and shape of the room, any adjoining spaces, and the window placements. Encourage customers to visualize themselves in that space, continuing to ask questions: *"What size furniture do you have?"* and *"How do you think your furniture would fit in here?"* Prompt them to mentally place their furniture and see how it makes them feel. Encouraging customers in this way strengthens their attachment to the space. The recurring theme in a perfect demonstration is to lead the customer to mentally move into the home.

## Outdoor Space

For many people, outdoor space is just as important as indoor space because. Therefore, also lead your customers out into the backyard so they may experience the outdoor living space as opposed to just viewing it from the windows from inside.

Even if the outdoor living space is unfinished, take them outside so they can get a rear view of the house. Have them envision a covered patio, deck, veranda, pool or any other options that may be available to them. Spending time in the backyard often helps future homeowners see the relationship to neighbors and the degree of privacy that they'll enjoy. Viewing the house from the outside is also a perfectly suitable opportunity to quickly discuss the gutters and downspouts, roofing materials, and any other feature that helps demonstrate the value and quality in how your homes are built. Outdoor space, especially from the backyard, grants an entirely different—and very telling—perspective of the home and property. It helps them imagine what it would be like if it were theirs.

## Storage Space

As you move through a model, draw attention to all of the storage space. Open every closet and show the customer how the space is conducive to their storage needs. Many people care deeply about how their home is organized and storage space is a huge part of that, whether in the form of a front entryway coat closet for guests or a hallway linen cabinet next to the bathroom or a master suite walk-in closet.

Help customers to envision how they would use each storage space as if they were living there. This is how you guide them to take ownership of the home. Though it may sound mundane, every single space plays into the home buying experience and builds upon the customer's decision-making process.

## Garage

The garage is often a very important part of the home and can be a true selling point for homebuyers. Although a garage is not considered part of the living square footage, there are many points of discussion that come along with this space. You can speak to whether or not the garage door is insulated; the ceiling and door opening heights; whether the garage is prewired for a door opener or if it is included; if there is a side door; and the number of included electrical outlets. If finished walls and a sealed floor are available, that makes a wonderful talking point especially for the buyer who likes the garage to be an attractive extension of the home. The garage is often an ideal place to talk about the foundation of your home, especially if it is post-tension concrete, for example. Even the simplest, potentially least glamorous room in the home is impressive when paying attention to the details and showing how every little thing really does matter.

## Under Construction: The Hard Hat Tour

If you happen to be selling homes that are yet to be built or under construction and you don't have a decorated model, focus on what you can show: how the building is built and the quality of construction and floorplan. Discuss the framing techniques, walls, foundation, plumbing pipes, electrical wiring and ductwork. Call direct attention to the brands used for each of these, as well as the brands of the heating and air conditioning unit, plumbing fixtures, wall paint, appliances, and so on. Moreover, show the energy-efficient features and benefits of each product as well as the brand guarantees and warranties. You don't need a completed home to sell value, quality and floor plan. In fact, a home under construction can often remind you and the customer of materials and items that are otherwise taken for granted.

Seize every opportunity to show customers how, when, where, and why you are creating the best possible buying—and living—experience for them by showing them what's inside your walls, in your attics and underground.

## Time to Site

Exceptional product knowledge empowers you to create wins for all parties involved. When you fully understand your company, the products you are promoting, the services you're representing, and the benefits of everything, you will know the proper questions to access customers' needs as they come up and will be well equipped to recommend the best possible solutions.

Once you've guided your new homebuyer through the model, offering a full demonstration of the qualities, features and benefits in and out, simply ask, *"What do you think about this home?"* And then listen. Listen to their feedback. Allow them to express their considerations and ask questions. Customers' responses are an indicator for how well you've done demonstrating the home and where your presentation should go next. At this point you ask, *"What do you think about this floor plan?"* and *"Is this a home you'd like to own?"* Then, just as you assumed permission to demonstrate the model, now it's time to assume permission to show the customer home sites—to help select the lot for the new home or to select the unit suite for the new condo. If the customer desires to move forward, match his or her enthusiasm and keep the momentum: *"Great, let's go look at the available home sites."*

## Recap

• The perfect demonstration includes guiding your customers through the home using all their senses, emphasizing sight and touch.

• Pay special attention to the floor plan configuration and the quality amenities used in the home. Speak to the features, benefits, brands and warranties.

• Slow customers down and lead them to experience the value across every room, in every space, with regard to every physical and experiential facet.

• As you move through your demonstration, ask test questions that will help you find out how well you're doing and gauge what the customer is thinking or feeling.

## Crucial Questions

• *"What do you think?"*
• *"How would you use and decorate this room? How do you think your furniture fit in here?"*
• *"What do you think of these features?"*
• *"What do you think about this home?"*
• *"Is this a home you'd like to own?"*
• *"Great, let's go look at the available home sites."*

# HOW TO STOMP THE COMPETITION

*"All is fair in love and war."*

– Francis Edward Smedley

**\*\*\*\***

*Early in my career I was selling a community in Elk Grove, California. I was young and enthusiastic, and very green. One day, a woman named Judy came in with a group of friends. Judy told me that she was looking for a home for her brother and his family. I asked questions about her brother and his family to further understand their needs and wants. I toured Judy and her friends through each of our models. After their visit, I followed up extensively with Judy to no avail. It wasn't until months later that I saw her larger-than-life image on the big screen at the MAME Awards and I learned that Judy was not a customer prospect at all, but my competition—and that she had mystery shopped me. At that moment, I realized that "All is fair in love and war"...and new home sales.*

**\*\*\*\***

## Do Your Due Diligence

There is one thing that every New Home Sales PROfessional should remember and that is: **D**o Your **D**ue **D**iligence, or the Three Ds. These days it isn't enough to just know *your* product inside and out. You must be an expert at knowing your competition as well.

In today's competitive marketplace, consumers are savvier than ever because they have easy access to information on the internet. People do their homework to ensure they get the best possible buy. When purchasing a new home, buyers want to feel that they are getting the greatest value for their money. Keeping up with these savvy, value-driven consumers means knowing all the features and benefits, or lack thereof, of your competition. Better position yourself professionally and help your customers make informed decisions. Knowledge is power and in the context of new home sales there is nothing that will serve you better than doing your due diligence by studying the competition.

## Types of Competition

Overall there are three types of competition for new homes. First, there is competition from other new homes. This sector accounts for the largest amount of competition, as these homes offer the most comparable options for consumers to choose from. Second, there is competition from resale homes. Third, there is competition from the customer's current home. When people are shopping for a new home, it is important not to discount the complacency they have with their current home.

With every type of competition there is a unique set of challenges to address. But, when it comes to knowing the competition, there are four areas of focus that will prove invaluable each and every time: People, Prices, Plans and Products.

## The Four Ps

### (Sales)People

The most important part of being able to stomp the competition from other new homes is knowing the competition's salespeople. Salespeople are absolutely instrumental in a customer's decision-making process when it comes to purchasing a new home. As the face of a company, you represent, not just how service-oriented a company is, but also the company's value, quality and integrity.

You must find out how well your competition sells. You must learn how your competition interacts with customers. You must find out how and how well your competition follows up with customers. Most importantly, you must discover what the competition says about *your* company and *your* homes. As any professional athlete in team sports knows, studying a competitor's people and how they play the game, is essential to countering attacks and gaining a positive advantage.

****

*Across the street from my Elk Grove community was another national home builder's community. We were consistently neck-and-neck in sales. After my experience with Judy, I decided to try my hand at mystery shopping and visited my competitor across the street.*

*I went on my day off in every-day clothes, with my hair pulled back and sunglasses on. I borrowed my sister's car and walked in like any other customer. My competitor, Patrick, promptly greeted me at his topo table and from there began his initial ABC presentation, telling me about the Area, the Builders and the Community. As part of his presentation, he walked me over to the aerial map and pointed out the schools, shopping centers, and parks, as well as his community's relationship to the freeways and major roads.*

*He then pointed to my community and emphasized how it backed right up against the train tracks! His community was across the street. Though there was no truly appreciable difference in noise level between the locations of our two communities, he had chosen one specific feature and used it to negatively differentiate his community from mine. He was, in effect, knocking my community as part of selling his own right in his initial presentation. This bit of information was more important than knowing anything about the competitor's pricing, incentives or amenities. Experiencing how he sold against us was the best piece of information I could get..*

*I was then able to take that small bit of knowledge and adjust my own presentation to highlight our location and how everybody loves the train which was evidenced by our sales success. In fact, our community plot map on the topo table had a real electric Lionel train set going around it.*

## Shopping the Competition

New home sales is an incredibly competitive, and rewarding, field that expects its professionals to be constantly on the front line, ready to win a sale. Shopping your competition prepares you for the win, informing you of customers' options and allowing you to be more attuned to what your customers may be looking for. Shopping the competition apprises you of the branding, marketing, modeling, touring and other related activities that are happening in your industry so that you can remain current and cutting-edge in your own practices.

*What does it mean to shop the competition?*

The average new home salesperson "shops" the competition by visiting competitors to pick up a price list, go through the models, and get a copy of the floor plans.

They often introduce themselves and the company that they work for. They may ask a few questions such as *"How many lots do you have?"* or *"How many homes have been sold?"* or *"What are your incentives?"* and then tour the models in minutes and be on their way. This method, however, only scratches the surface in terms of obtaining useful information. When you shop the competition, make it a matter of reconnaissance, conducted incognito. Otherwise you give yourself away.

If you arrive at a competitor's model home in the nice fancy car you take clients around in, or if you walk in wearing your business clothes and company nametag, you are telling your competitors exactly who you are and thereby miss the opportunity to gain better inside information. If they identify you as a competitor, they are only going to tell or show you what they are willing to let you know, which is essentially what you could already find in the company's brochure, on the price list and online. What you want to obtain is the in-depth information that prospects are given.

Here are some tips: Go on your days off. If you have the option, forego the luxury car and take a less obvious make and model. Show up in blue jeans and comfortable shoes and a T-shirt. Hide behind sunglasses or other accessories if you are more likely to be recognized. Devise a story complete with a fake name, place of work, current residential location, family structure, reason for moving—all of the answers to all of the typical questions that would be asked by new home salespeople so that your story comes out smoothly. Even go so far as to establish an anonymous email address that you can provide to the communities you visit so you can track competitors' follow-up practices. This type of preparedness in your reconnaissance will grant you access to such incredible benefits in understanding the competition.

****

When shopping the competition incognito, you obtain a more honest portrait of the competition. You learn whether or not the salesperson makes an effort to greet customers, shakes hands, asks questions, and tours customers through the models. You find out how personable they are. Shopping the competition serves as powerful motivation with regard to what other new home sales businesses do or, more often, don't do. By knowing what competitors don't do, you can rest assured that if you do everything you're supposed to, you will have the advantage.[*]

*Prices*

A builder's pricing structure, including its upgrade options, is another important aspect of doing your due diligence. Upfront and embedded costs are what determine a buyer's ability to successfully a desired

---

[*] If you have questions or concerns about mystery shopping your competition, feel free to call me at (916) 768-5525 for a no cost consultation.

property. Customers are constantly trying to determine which new home is the best value for the money. Being able to informatively speak your customers about a competitor's option pricing is extremely helpful in assisting them in making comparisons between your homes and other builders'. This is especially true if your homes are higher priced but include upgrades as standard features. So, as you are out conducting your mystery shopping, try to get their option prices.

At this point you may be thinking that what I am suggesting this is really extreme and maybe even cutthroat. I don't think it is. Admittedly, though, it is extremely competitive. But, just like all builders are required to make their disclosures available to prospects prior to purchasing, their option pricing should be available to prior to purchasing. If you and your company are losing sales to a competitor, compare apples to apples and access the total price of the home with the extras. Many of your customers do, especially the analytical ones.

*Plans*

When comparing information with competitors, it is important to obtain copies of the floor plans. Make notes about how the floor plans differ from yours. This means looking at features that are or are not included in each, considering whether a floor plan's design make sense and either add to or detract from its value, and understanding how furniture layout and design dynamics influence livability. It is critical that you be able to knowledgably speak to such characteristics with customers.

*Products*

Picking up a competitor's features list, or taking notes about the competition's products, is also useful in sizing up the competition. Different product brands carry different weight with consumer audiences. By becoming well versed in a competitor's product choices, you are better able to address customers' questions regarding warranties and benefits, and how a product's features relate to the expectations customers have for their future homes. By adhering to the Four Ps, and Three Ds, you can successfully shop—and stomp—your competition.

*Take Pictures*

As referenced in the description of the Four Ps, gather the floor plans, product lists and price lists but also take a multitude of color photos as you tour models, capturing every feature you can.

One reason for taking pictures is to help you remember the details of your competitors' homes. As you go out and shop different competitors, it is important that you be able to recall specifics and attribute features accurately. As you work closely with customers, it will help if you can speak to other properties in a well-versed way. When shopping the competition, spend as much time as you need to in different builders' model homes, examining their floor plans and taking pictures, as well as taking notes on the décor to assist in defining and differentiating the properties.

Chances are the buyers also are going to remember the décor before they remember the square footage or plan name. It is imperative to make notes about where your comparable plans are distinctive so that you can readily address customers' points of interest.

As a way of organizing the specs you gather, photos you take and notes you make, keep an updated competition book at all times. The purpose of these competition books is to literally show customers—and not just tell—how your properties compare. Having tangible samples of competitor-defined information and imagery is a compelling way to engage customers in a comparison of quality and value with regard to your own community. It is challenging to remember every feature of every builder's products and plans, but with the information at your fingertips you are equipped to conduct side-by-side comparisons with your homebuyers. Knowing what other options customers are exploring is vital to your ability to sell your homes.

Keeping a detailed consumer-oriented competition book will serve you in converting more prospects—especially analytical clients who desire all the facts. Always be prepared to help customers compare. That's one of the undeniable characteristics of a true new home sales expert!

## Competing with Resale Homes

When engaging with customers, it is important to get a sense of what other options they are considering. Ask your customers *"Are there any other home builders that you are considering seriously?"* If you are walking them through your models, excuse yourself and give them some time to enjoy them on their own. Go back to your sales office and review your file and notes so you are prepared to respond to their questions.

Beyond knowing the finer points of your specific competitors and their new homes, you must also have a working knowledge of other aspects of the housing industry. Your customers may be interested in similar new home opportunities, but they may also be exploring resale homes.

Knowing the resale market is part and parcel of stomping the competition in today's marketplace. You have to know what to look for—such as the length of time a property has been listed, any changes in price, whether a property's features and amenities have been updated recently. Incorporate resale properties into your competition books and be prepared to ask your customers questions like, *"Have you thought about how much it will cost you to update, repair, repaint, re-carpet or re-landscape a pre-existing property?"*

Most brand new homes are relatively comparable to homes that are less than 10 years old. If you do not have access to a Multiple Listing Service (MLS) for your area, you should definitely get it. Many home builders overlook this import source of information. When you have access to the resale homes listed in your area, you can track the sales rates and prices at which resale homes are selling, as well as additional information on new home competition.

When it comes to working with your customer, it is your responsibility to provide the best customer sales service by assisting customers in comparing your homes to any that they may be considering. Winning a customer over requires generating examples of how the features of your home benefit the customer as opposed to those of the competition, and doing so without knocking the competition so as not to insult the customer's choices.

Be sure to stress the benefits of your new homes, and to illustrate how a new home allows customers to feel confident in what they are getting—they are purchasing a home that isn't mired in issues from age or neglect. If you have all the comparative information at your fingertips, you can openly, honestly discuss options in a way that doesn't impinge on your customer's interests but that positively highlights your new home.

## Recap

• Follow the Three Ds: **D**o Your **D**ue **D**iligence. Conduct research and do your homework.

• Shop the competition and study their Four Ps: **P**eople, **P**rices, **P**lans and **P**roducts. Preparation is the key.

• Thoroughly review your competitors and compile your competition books so that you have a full suite of information at your fingertips that will help you demonstrate the superiority of your home.

• As you guide your customers through the decision-making process, uncover what your customers are considering seriously by asking questions.

## Crucial Questions

• "Do I know the competition's people, prices, plans and products?"
• "Am I being strategic and deliberate in how I'm shopping the competition?
• "Do I have a good cover and the story and contact info to support it?"
• *"Are there any other home builders that you are considering seriously?"*
• *"Have you thought about how much it may cost you to update a pre-existing property?"*

# CONTENDING WITH CONTINGENCIES

*"Do they have a house to sell?"*

*– Every New Home Sales Manager Ever*

*I remember working on the front lines as a new home salesperson and that incredible feeling of landing a sale and the predictable question from management: "Do they have a house to sell?" One of the first things my boss wanted to know about each sale was whether or not the customer was contingent. That question of whether or not a sale is viable—and more so, "Will it count for this quarter" or "Will it close by fiscal year-end?"—is always a big one in new home sales. Customers wonder if they really will be able to buy the new home. Builders wonder if they really should start building a home. The national builders wonder if they will meet earnings estimates. Stockholders wonder if they will receive a good return on investment.*

*Throughout my career, I have identified several best practices to access the probability of whether a customer's home will sell and close quickly and thereby increase the probability that the new home will close escrow on their new home immediately upon completion.*

\*\*\*\*

Your ability to garner viable sales that close on time is paramount to providing both your company and your customers with the best possible service. The sale timeframe of your customer's current home is a significant part of doing just that. Contingencies can make or break a deal. You have to do everything you can to support your customers in getting their homes sold *fast*. Taking a contingency where the home is overpriced is a waste of time, energy and money for all parties involved.

## Ask the Customer Questions

Filling in the details is essential when you have a customer who has decided to move forward with the purchase of one of your new homes but has a home to sell first. Ask to-the-point questions that will inform you right up front of the conditions you're dealing with. *"When did you buy your home?"* to find out how long ago they bought it; *"How old is the home?"* to assess what factors and features may affect the sale of it; and *"What did you pay for it?"* so you can gauge whether or not your customers have enough equity in their home to sell it.

Asking what someone paid for a house may feel slightly uncomfortable, but this is a time when you have to really dare to dig. In most cases, a homebuyer's ability to complete the new home purchase is completely contingent upon the successful close of escrow of his or her current home, which means that equity is a huge factor. You may also want to ask customers if they've taken any cash out on their home, or if there is a second mortgage or equity line of credit against the home: *"How much do you owe on it?"* And after you've gotten a sense for someone's current home and financial status, ask follow-up questions that give you a sense of what the customer is thinking: *"How much do you think it's worth in today's marketplace?"* and *"Have you calculated how much you may net from the sale of your home?"*

When it comes to contingency sales, one of the most important questions to ask is *"Are you willing to price your home to sell within 30 days?"* The ideal timeline for selling a contingent home is 30 days. This should be the standard practice regardless of when the new home in your community will be complete. Most contingent addendums in purchase agreements are on a 30-day basis, so you want to prime customers for that and ask them if indeed they want to sell within that timeframe. If the customer is comfortable with a 30-day sale, you must also ask, *"If needed, would you be willing to lower the price of your home to get it sold in time to make this purchase happen?"* It is imperative that you know the customer's willingness and ability in to lower the sale price.

## Gather Information

### Net Sheet

A great resource to gather financial information about a customer's current home is the net sheet. Filled out by the listing agent, the net sheet shows the probable sales price of the home less all of the costs to sell. Although it varies state to state, the general rule for the cost to sell includes approximately six percent in real estate commission, two percent in title, escrow and/or attorney's fee, and some price discount. Typically, an owner's cost to sell will total anywhere between eight and ten percent of the purchase price. Taking that percentage, subtract it and the amount a customer owes on the home from the sales price of the house to get an approximation of how much money he or she will likely walk away with. This, of course, assumes that the home is priced right to begin with and doesn't need to be reduced in order to sell.

### MLS Listing

Multiple Listing Service (MLS) will most likely be your primary resource for doing your own competitive market analysis (CMA) of your customer's listing. Typical contingency addendums require the customer's listing agent to provide you with a copy of the subject property's MLS printout, as well as three comparable sales.

Although the realtor will most likely provide you with accurate sold comps, take it upon yourself to verify the information. Homes can vary so much in price range that you want to make sure you have a realistic feel for what is happening in the marketplace. The MLS will give you insight into whether the listing is likely to sell in a timely manner. Some of the key items of information found on the MLS listing include the price point for the customer's current home, the year it was built, the total number of days it has been on the market, the total square footage and the price per square foot. All of these figures provide a great at-a-glance understanding of your customer's current home.


## Analyze

Although the property listing, as well as the net sheet, is a valuable resource, it cannot tell the whole story in and of itself. To confirm a viable sale in your community, you have to analyze the listing of your customer's current home within the market context. The best venue to do so is through your local MLS, though other resources such as realtor.com, the National Association of Realtors website, can also provide great access to marketplace information.

Simply ensure that the resources you use grant you a full picture of your customer's home and its position within the housing market relative to other homes.

The first way to ascertain whether a home is listed right is to review the other active homes listed for sale within the same area. At the height of the real estate boom, the determining factor for whether or not a home would sell was location, location, location. But in today's marketplace—as is true of any time a market is downward trending or flat—the determining factor of whether or not a home sells is price, price, price. How a home is priced compared to what it's competing against is the number one determination in whether or not a home sells. Be sure to share that with your customers.

In addition to the active homes, including REOs and short sales, evaluate the pending sales and sold/closed comps to estimate what your customer's home may actually appraise for. Appraisal issues are one of the leading problems in terms of getting a buyer's financing to close so your escrow can close on time. Conducting a price analysis of homes sold will help you to verify whether or not the home is actually priced right to sell.

One final point of analysis is to review MLS comments and look at the overall marketing for the property. You want to ensure your homebuyer's current property shines within MLS because the listing really is the top tool used to market homes in the agent comments.

Ask the customer and realtor to share their overall marketing program so you have a sense of the property's visibility, reach, and presence within the market. Criteria to look for include the quantity and quality of photos of the home; whether the MLS form is completely filled out so that all of the home's features are included—down to details such as what direction the home faces; and the listing agent's remarks. In representing the future interest of your purchaser, support the listing agent in putting his or her best foot forward on the listing. Agent remarks provide a great platform for thoroughly describing the property and making a great sales pitch. Your customer needs that property description to be completely filled out with details that will entice buyers. Help the agent incorporate some key words that will jump out at customers or suggest fully capitalized text to make a heading appear bold, thus making the MLS listing stand out compared to others. These are small tricks but they will make a big difference.

Always be respectful of the listing agent's work but also be willing to share your ideas with them. Your perspective and input may serve to enhance the property's standing and better achieve the results needed to fulfill the contingency expectations of your builder.

Sample Analysis

The first step in analyzing a home and how it is situated within the market is to pull up active comps within the same zip code region. If a customer's home is priced at $245,000 you want to pick a price range in which that figure comfortably fits, such as $200-250,000, to search for comps. Next, take into account the year the customer's home was built. If a home was built in 2007, pick a 10-year timeframe around then, such as 2001-2011. If you go much older than five or so years, the home isn't quite as comparable. Searching relevant ranges for price and year built is a quick way to assess how much competition there is in terms of the number of other homes on the market. If you get a large number, especially be sure to narrow the results to only the regular active listings to start. It's also important to look at properties listed within the last 90 days to get an accurate picture of how the market is moving.

As you conduct this refined search, take a quick snapshot of the stats so you can see the averages of the active listings. Take, for example, your customer's $245,000 listing: approximately 1,800 square feet, at around $135 per square foot, on the market for 30 days. After conducting a search, you find other available listings that average 2,000 square feet, at only $115 per square foot, and have been on the market 50 days! This grants you a comprehensive view of the market and very telling indictors that your customer's home may be overpriced.

Once you have narrowed your list of properties to choose from and found out the averages relevant to your customer's home, find a similar property to compare. As you look for a parallel property, pay attention to key features of your customer's home, such as whether the house is single-story or multi-level. At this point you should have already viewed the pictures for your customer's property so you know what kind of features the home possesses. Using the images posted on a listing is a great way to compare properties to each other.

You can deduce information based on the exterior appearance, cabinets and countertops, flooring, wall paint and trim, and more. This will help you investigate the physical and aesthetic features that play into peoples' perceived value of each property.

How well a home shows and how well it is marketed are certainly critical to selling successfully, but nothing trumps price. At a time when short sales and REOs flood the market, comps are more difficult to pin down. One way agents price short sales is to place them below the last sold comp in an area, dropping as much as 10 percent off the price in order to sell more quickly. For a home priced at $250,000, that's an instant drop of $25,000. When that sort of drop occurs repeatedly, it creates a downward price shift that makes it difficult to list a house competitively which is an important factor to consider as customers try and sell their homes and purchase new.

You want to find out what homes are selling for—what your buyer's current home is competing against—across all listing types. The fact of the matter is that when an appraiser goes to appraise a property, its status as a regular sale or a short sale won't affect the value it's assigned—and it shouldn't! Sold comps can often grant an illuminating view of the market activity. When looking at sold homes you want to apply the same criteria as before in terms of zip code, age range, price per square foot, and days on the market. You don't necessarily need to get specific in terms of controlling for number of bedrooms or even total square footage because price will be the most important factor. Focus on using sold properties to further your understanding of how quickly current listings are selling.

You have to take regular actives, REOs, foreclosures, short sales, and sold homes all into consideration as you evaluate your customer's listing and measure whether your own community has a viable sale that's likely to close on time. When it comes to contingencies, evaluate a buyer's listing and work in conjunction with the listing agent to make sure the home is priced for today's marketplace and will get sold.

## Bump or Sell Over

Once you've done the homework on your buyer's current home and how it compares to similar properties on the market, assess the situation and make a realistic decision about whether or not to sell over your buyer's lot. If there are other homes with clearly motivated sellers, pricing at a substantially lower price per square foot than your customer is willing to go, the timely sale of your customer's home is a lot less likely. Not only is an overpriced home a disservice to the home seller but, even if it does sell, it won't appraise at an inflated value.

It's important to give customers a shot—to extend the benefit of the doubt to begin with, but be mindful of the reality. If your assessment reveals that your customer's home is not likely to sell, bump the first buyer with another non-contingent buyer. The only reason to keep someone on a lot who doesn't have great initial prospects for the current home is if he or she is willing to lower the price significantly. That's where the final question comes in: *"Are you willing to lower your price enough to make this sale happen?"*

The bottom line is whether or not your homebuyer is willing to do what it takes to make it happen—willing to lower the price enough to sell in today's marketplace and get the new purchase to go through. As you work with your customers to support the sale of their current home, apprise them of their options. One of your responsibilities is to help coordinate concurrent closes. Reach out to your customer and his or her listing agent to see about negotiating a rent-back or similar scenario. This will enable the seller—your purchaser—to sell the house and close escrow, but continue to live in the house for a short period to allow enough time to move.

## Close the Contingency

Being a true Sales PROfessional means that your company can count on you, can count on your sales. Your company has to be able to know that if you write a contingency, you're going to work with the home seller and listing agent to do what it takes to get the current home sold so that your sale is a viable one that can be counted on the books.

Part of your responsibility to your company is having accurate assessments and accurate numbers in the backlog. This includes contingencies—reporting cancellations but also selling over contingencies if that's what needs to be done. Always try and make it happen for your customer by being proactive. This means having the price conversation with your customers early on and doing your homework to support a competitive price. Remember, though, that at the end of the day your goal should be to solidify closed sales for your customers, your company and yourself.

The faster the customer sells their home, the faster they can have peace of mind that they are indeed moving forward with the new home and can start packing. The faster the customer's home sells, the faster the builder can count on the closing and the anticipated earnings. The faster you create wins for all stakeholders.

### Recap

• Evaluate the viability of your contingencies by conducting your own analysis of all active listings—including regular actives, REOs, short sales, and foreclosures.

• Plan on selling over your contingencies if you have another ready, willing, able buyer. When you take a contingency, keep the new home on the market in the event that you have to sell over and be sure to alert your customer to any stipulating clause in which 30 days (or a similar timeframe) is allotted for sale of the home.

### Crucial Questions

• *"Where do you live now? Do you own or rent?"*
• *"What do you plan to do with your current home when you purchase a new one?*
• *"When did you buy your home? How old is your home?"*
• *"What did you pay for it?"*
• *"How much do you owe on it?"*
• *"What do you think your house is worth in today's marketplace?"*
• *"Have you calculated how much you'd net from the sale of your home?"*
• *"Are you willing to price your home to sell 30 days?"*
• *"Do you have it on the market yet?"*
• *"Do you have a second mortgage on your home?*
• *"If needed, would you be willing to lower the price of your home to get it sold in time to make the purchase happen?*
• *"If needed, would you be willing to bring money to the table?"*
• *"If you allowed for a foreclosure or short sale, do you have a family member who would purchase a new home for you?"*

# OVERCOMING OBJECTIONS

*"Show people what they want most, and they will move heaven and earth to get it."*

– Frank Bettger

## Today's Marketplace

Today's economy presents an environment in which many people and industries are working to get back to a place of stability. Within the recovering housing market, builders are finding themselves having to spar with each other for competitive prices and incentives that will attract customers. At the same time, many customers either find themselves with financial complications or are wary of the market, or both. As a result, customers present additional challenges for new home salespeople to overcome in order to make the sale and close the deal.

A further complication of customer objections is that an individual's reasons for objecting aren't always readily apparent. This means that you, as the sales PROfessional, have to know the right questions to ask—and how to ask them—to uncover what customers are really thinking and feeling.

This is the first step to understanding what a customer's objection is based on. Beyond knowing what kind of questions to ask, it is important to have some techniques handy that directly address the different types of objections. This will allow you to better understand where your customers are coming from and help them through their decision-making process. Only once you overcome your customers' objections can you move the sale forward today.

## Objections are Opportunities

Before addressing the specific types of objections and techniques that can be employed to assuage them, it's important to understand what an objection represents in the mind of a customer. Any customer's objection is grounded in real thoughts and feelings, which means the new home salesperson has to be sensitive to what the customer is expressing—being both understanding and respectful. What is to understand about objections, though, is that they are also signs of interest. The very fact that a customer voices an objection is a sign that he or she is considering how to make a new home purchase happen.

When a customer expresses an objection it typically means that he or she is sharing a concern that needs to be satisfied. They are cluing you in to something that is holding him or her back. An objection signifies that a customer needs more information in order to move forward.

For you, a customer's objection is an opportunity. It is an opportunity for you to satisfy a customer's concern, to present the right information for a customer to take the next step in the sales experience. Ultimately, an objection is a customer's way of telling you how to sell them, which is why it is imperative that you listen, and listen really well. Your role is to facilitate the customer overcoming his or her own objection. To ensure your ability to help your customer, there are three primary steps to follow.

*Step 1: Embrace the Objection*

When you hear an objection from a customer, the first thing you need to do is embrace what it is the customer is saying, even if you don't completely understand where they are coming from.

Clear understanding is absolutely the key to overcoming any and all objections. Never ignore or avoid an objection because a customer's ability to surmount an objection is the only way to advance the purchase of a new home. Instead, explore the objection. Find out what's holding them back from purchasing. One of the fears that I hear sales people express is that they don't want to pry. Additionally, they don't want to come across as pushy. They don't want to be nosey. So they don't dig deeper in what are probably the more sensitive, personal issues for the customer. But, what I want to suggest is that it is okay to ask personal questions. It's just more of a matter of *how* you ask those questions.

## Step 2: Empathize

Listening is the primary principle in empathizing with a customer. It is not uncommon for customers to hold back their real reasons for objecting, either out of discomfort, embarrassment, or some other factor. To embrace a customer's objection, you have to listen carefully for what a customer is *not* telling you as much as what is being said. More so, you have to listen intently and openly. Each customer is different. It is only by listening to what each one has to say that you can truly understand where individuals are coming from.

In reaching a place of empathy with your customers, you also want to ask questions in response to what you hear them saying. This will grant you a clearer understanding of a customer's perspective and help you see all aspects of the concern.

What you know or think or feel is secondary to the customer's perspective, for a customer's point-of-view is what will teach you what you need to talk about and show to help the customer—and the sale—move forward. Asking questions is a way to think about where the customer is coming from as you hone in on an objection's point of origin. In empathizing with a customer, you will be better equipped to identify an individual's objection, invite dialogue about the objection, and uncover a customer's real reasons for objecting. From there, you can tailor a response that suits his or her specific needs.

*Step 3: Present a Solution*

After embracing and empathizing with a customer's objection you should be prepared to present the customer with a solution. For most customers, buying a home is like a jigsaw puzzle, they are trying to put the pieces together to make it work. As the facilitator of the solving process, your job is to help each customer find the missing piece and put the puzzle together.

Upon gathering the requisite information and carefully considering the needs of your customer, formulate a solution that appropriately addresses his or her concerns. In doing so, you'll be able to overcome any objection to help them move forward.

*Mindset and Attitude*

Part of turning customers' objections into opportunities is adopting a mindset and attitude for yourself in which you see the possibilities. To help you do so, there is one central thing to understand about the customers you come into contact with who voice objections: If a customer is out looking at homes, he or she is there for a reason. It is your job to find out what that reason is and tap into the customer's motivations.

Your mindset and attitude will inform your ability to help customers overcome their objections, and will also set the stage for customers' mindsets and attitudes as they seek to find a way to buy the homes they want and need today.

The surest way to be an effective sales PROfessional—mastering the steps and effectively employing the techniques to overcome objections—is to cultivate in yourself the positivity and proactivity that you wish to see in your customers.

*Techniques for Overcoming Objections*

Specific techniques can be employed to further break down the three-step framework for turning objections into opportunities. First, anticipate an objection before it arises. Likewise, draw out an objection once you sense a customer has one. If the objection isn't entirely clear, you want to isolate it by asking questions. Questions are critical to overcoming objections. From there you want to provide a solution, or solutions, to the objection. Further, have third-party endorsements and some personal stories on hand to serve as supplementary techniques for gaining the customer buy-in you need to move the sale forward. These last two will help you create commonality with the customer's experience, giving them experiences they can relate to. Though each objection is different, these techniques work well within the three steps to address even the toughest customer objections.

## Six Tough Objections

Customer objections can vary in size and scope, but there are certain ones that comprise the majority of customer concern as you engage people in the home-buying process. Based on industry experience, the following seven objectives are the toughest obstacles new home salespeople face today:

#1: *Credit issues*: There are a lot of buyers out there with credit issues.

#2: *No down payment*: Some people are still saving the cash needed to meet down payment and closing cost requirements.

#3: *Get a better deal*: There are a lot of customers out there who think they can get a better deal and want to keep shopping to see if they can find it.

#4: *Market timing and price decline*: Customers often think they should wait to see if prices will fall more.

#5: *Lack of urgency*: There are some customers who have no clear reason to buy, which can make their needs difficult to address.

#6 *Need to think about it:* Many customers say they need to think about a purchase more as a way of avoiding making a decision.

These six objections represent the greatest, most relevant obstacles in new home sales today. Even as obstacles, though, these objections are not insurmountable. Each one can be openly and proactively addresses to support customers in moving forward with the purchase of a new home sooner rather than later.

### Credit Issues

When it comes to credit issues, you want to bring out the objection right away. It's okay to simply ask, *"Do you plan on financing the home?" "Have you talked to a lender yet?" "How much did they say you could quality for?" "How's your credit?"* and *"Do you know your FICO scores?"*

Don't hesitate to find out a customer's credit-related history. The economic downturn could have affected a customer's credit in multiple ways, which is information you need to know up front if a customer is interested in moving forward. *"Have you had a bankruptcy, foreclosure or short sale within the last two years?"* Dare to dig on this topic: *"How's your credit been since then? Have you had any late payments of more than 30 days in the last two years?"* You want people to tell you about the issues they've been having. It's one of the only ways to clarify financial standing in terms of eligibility to buy.

If your customer has credit issues, ask him or her to tell you about it, and offer your support: *"Maybe I can help."* Make sure you know what credit scores will qualify people for different types of loans, whether it is a credit score of 620 for a FHA loan with three and a half percent down or a score as low as 580 with five percent down on a FHA loan. Know what financing options are available for people with different scores. If there aren't any immediately feasible options, have the heart to ask: *"Have you considered working with a credit professional?"* Help your customer get the help they need to improve his or her score.

There are small ideas you can provide to your customers, such as calling credit card companies to renegotiate interest rates. You also can encourage them to pay a little bit extra on their monthly bills, which will help them stay on top of their debt and other financial commitments so they can focus on home-buying funds. And if overspending seems to be an issue, you can encourage them to cut up their credit cards, which will be an effective deterrent to spending, and thus an effective means of reducing expenses. Although these are not major solutions, they will help ease the financial burden of your customers.

As previously mentioned, one significant way you can help customers who have credit issues that keep them from moving forward with a purchase is to maintain a relationship with a reputable credit repair professional.

If your company doesn't already partner with such a service, find someone who you can trust and rely on to give you the truth when it comes to your customers, and who will do what it takes to work with your customers to repair their credit. Refer clients in need to your credit repair professional and follow up with both the customer and credit repair professional on a regular basis. As a sales PROfessional, show your customers how invested you are in their ability to purchase a home by helping to hold them accountable for repairing their credit.

Although credit repair is not always a quick, simple fix—which means that customers who need to repair their credit may not be able to purchase immediately—there is a potential long-term benefit to helping your customers with their credit problems. Think of it this way: If each month you connect one ineligible customer with a credit professional, after a year of meeting each you may have 12 customers who are ready and able to buy, and who are committed to you because you committed to them. Stick with your customers, and they will stick with you. When it comes to customers with credit issues, think in the long term. In six months or a year, you could see a substantial increase in your income just by sticking with customers who initially had no obvious ability to obtain financing for the home. Stick with your future prospects and they will stick with you. Remember, it's the little things that make a difference in your sales success.

*No Down Payment*

Similar to bad credit, you want to find out about a down payment objection right in front. *"How much money do you have saved for your down payment and closing costs?"* When asking about the down payment, be sure to include closing costs in the discussion because both have to be provided right up front. *"Where is your down payment coming from?"* You always want to know where the money is—a bank account or in savings? That's a huge question for lenders. Ask, *"Where is that money coming now?"* and *"Do you have access to any gift funds?"* to find out the details. You can ask customers about their 401k or retirement plans: *"How do you feel about tapping into your 401k to invest in a home?"* For many retirement plans there are no penalties for borrowing against it or early withdrawal to purchase a home purchase, especially for first-time buyers.

If a customer just needs to come up with the last couple thousand, you also may want to suggest to your customers adjusting their tax withholdings. *"Did you know that you can adjust your withholdings and bring home more money each month?"* Your customer could make a temporary adjustment to have more money coming in each month to apply to their down payment, and then change it back once escrow is closed. If the customer isn't interested in these options, but is still saving for a home purchase, ask *"How much can you save per month toward your down payment?"* And, whenever you are discussing the feasibility of a purchase, ask your customer *"Are you willing to do what it takes to make this home yours?"*

If you get a *"Yes"* from your customer then you want to start suggesting possible solutions. First, there are low- or no-down payment loans—USDA can be zero down and FHA can be three and a half percent, which really isn't that much money. For example, on a $200,000 home a customer only needs about $6,600, which most people can scrounge up over time. Just like with credit issues, you want to think longer term for people who don't have the down payment burning a hole in their pockets.

If the customer needs more time to gather a down payment, consider whether you can place him or her in a to-be-built home. If you're in a community where you've got enough lots to be there for a year, match a customer with a to-be-built home. You can even speak with your management about releasing one that's not released yet. Either way, you'll be providing the customer something to strive for and work toward. Once customers have signed a purchase agreement, they are so much more committed to doing what it takes to make it go through. In fact, all stakeholders are more committed—the salesperson, buyer, lender, and credit repair person—because they have a common goal to attain.

## Getting a Better Deal

One of the more challenging objections today is when customers assert that they can get a better deal. The housing market today is very price-driven which can make it challenging for companies to compete. Some builders are taking down lot premiums, while other builders who have larger homes with more amenities are dipping into lower price ranges where they can market their homes to customers as being a better overall value. Resale properties also need to be taken into account, especially those that are less than ten years old.

Although many marketplaces have flattened out and are no longer fighting tooth and nail in the same way they were, some places are still experiencing downward trends and inflated customer incentives remain. The level of competition makes it important for sales professionals to ask customers right up front what other locations, communities or homes they're considering. You want to know who and what you are competing against: *"What other homes are you considering seriously?"* Also ask your customers why they haven't bought yet if they're seeing better deals elsewhere: "*What was lacking that you didn't purchase it?*" You have to find out this kind of information, especially when it comes to negotiating. Customers won't necessarily share it with you until you ask for specifics.

The point is to understand where the customer is coming from, and to get a sense for what other new home builders are offering. Part of this is mystery shopping the competition yourself. You shouldn't just rely on what the customers are telling you—you need to be able to contextualize what it is they're saying. Learn for yourself what offers are out there in terms of prices, amenities, incentives and more.

As you try to set your homes apart, ask your customers, "*Of all the homes you've seen so far, how does ours compare?*" You want to know how well the customer likes your home and how badly he or she wants to own it. Their responses will tell you what angles you need to play to heighten the appeal for your customer, and you can transition into a professional presentation in which you can thoroughly demonstrate the value of your home. Customers need to know and understand what they'll get out of your homes that they won't get from the competition, whether it's the quality features, energy efficiency, product warranties or other factors.

Your ability to illustrate to customers the benefits throughout the home will help them see what they stand to gain. It isn't enough to say— you have to show to give the customer the full effect. Differentiate yourself from the competition by taking the opportunity to demonstrate to customers how the benefits of your home directly correlate to comfort and convenience in their lives, how the benefits directly address their life needs.

When faced with a customer objection related to getting a better deal, it's really important to first treat the concern fairly, and then to isolate the concern in terms of how you can resolve it. Address the objection empathetically: "*I can totally appreciate wanting to get a great deal on a home, and you should. And I will help you with that.*" Make sure that your house is indeed the one that the customer wants to own.

Once you've established the desire to purchase, make sure you know exactly why the customer wants your home, why it perfectly suits his or her needs and wants. After you've received confirmation that your house is what the customer wants, ask your customer, "*If you got a great deal on this home, would you buy it today?*" In following this line of questioning, you will find the strength of your position to negotiate.

When it comes to striking a deal, one of your responsibilities as the frontline salesperson is to meet the needs of your customer with the expectations of your builder. Part of mystery shopping the competition is to have proof of other builders' prices, amenities and incentives that will help gain your management's approval of any offers they may accept.

Any verifiable proof you can provide will make management more comfortable with any price discounts you present. Just as you advocate on behalf of your customer to your company, be prepared to advocate on behalf of your company. Ask the customer, "*If the company is willing to accept your offer, how much would you be willing to give in the way of additional earnest money deposit?*" If your company is going to give a concession, as a good faith gesture, you need to have some return assurance from the customer. Additionally, obtain unconditional loan approval as promptly as possible so the company can effectively hold the customer accountable for completing the purchase. Obtaining additional deposits solidifies the customer's commitment to the purchase. Additionally, it also helps to avoid last-minute renegotiations at the end of escrow and prevents buyer default. The point is to ask your customers what they're willing to do in exchange for a concession and make sure they take the necessary steps to match what your company accepts.

Striking deals with customers, even if it means making certain concessions in price or otherwise, can be a great way to get your company the business it needs. In any tough, competitive, or downward trending market, the first company to sell out wins. You will make the most money for your builder the faster you sell the homes. It's all about doing what you need to do to get your customers and your builder the results that work for them.

*Market Timing and Price Decline*

Objections about price decline are similar to those related to getting a better deal. The difference is that rather than assuming there is a better option right now, customers are inclined to wait and see if better circumstances arise. As a result of the recent economic downturn, some people are wondering if the economy will slide further, or have simply resigned themselves to an original investment being longer term than hoped for or expected.

When customers raise conversation about market timing and price decline, you want to anticipate an objection. Be proactive and ask your customers, *"What do you think about the market? How do you think it compares to three to five years ago?"* As an informed New Home Sales PROfessional, you already know how the market is in comparison.

It's much better in many ways, especially from a buyer's perspective, because prices are lower and interest rates are lower. The reason you ask customers questions is to help guide their thinking and move them toward a favorable conclusion. *"What do you think about today's prices? Have you seen how low interest rates are?"* You can even go so far as to ask, *"Do you believe that now might be the time to buy?"*

Belief is huge in customers overcoming objections, and that belief begins with you. So much of what happens in you is transferred to your customers. As a frontline Sales PROfessional, you can have the single greatest effect on the thinking and feeling of your customers. If you believe that now is the time to buy, that will translate to your customers and help them in their decision-making process.

Although your knowledge and opinion of price points and market timing will have a marked affect on your customers, you can certainly draw on other resources to support your claim. Keep up-to-date on news stories and market information that serve as third-party endorsements of favorable real estate market conditions that support the premise that now's the time to buy.

You will of course hope that conditions are going your way, but even if they aren't, you can still convince buyers that now is the time to buy. Begin by honoring your customer's concern: *"You're right, prices may decline even further, but look how good they are right now."* One compelling argument you can make is that interest rates are most likely not going to get any lower than they already are. Though prices may decline, you can frame customer advantages in terms of interest rate. Take, for example, a $300,000 home on which the interest rate increases a modest half percent, going from three and a half to four. That translates to an additional $34,000 in interest over the life of a loan, which is not necessarily a small number for customers who are concerned with total amounts. It can certainly be argued that low interest rates trump price decline. If your customers are looking for long-term ownership, they're better off locking in a low interest rate than waiting to see if prices will fall further. That's just one of the reasonable justifications you can provide your customers with to make sense of any concerns they have about market timing and price decline.

## Lack of Urgency

Many customers' objections manifest as a lack of urgency. Some buyers feel the need to look at everything on the market. Others say, *"If it's meant to be, it'll still be there when I'm ready to purchase."* Other customers are just afraid to buy.

When you find that you have a customer who lacks urgency, start with basic questions: *"What's your timeline for buying?"* And follow up the last question with, *"What's your timeline based on?"* You always want to find out what a customer's timeline is based on—the sale of a current home, the need to save more money, the fulfillment of a lease or...? The reason you want to find out what their timeline is based on is so you can determine if there is a way to move their timeline up. Remember, the mindset that "There's always a reason to buy right now, here, today." It's just your job to find out what that reason is for the customer. Or a customer's answer could imply readiness at any time if the right house is found, in which case you want to draw that out: *"If you found the perfect home today, when would you buy it?"* You can magnify urgency without being too pushy: *"I'm just curious, but if you don't mind me asking, what are you waiting for?"*

As you retrieve these answers from your customer, think about what information could tap into his or her need to buy sooner rather than later. Find out how much a customer is currently paying in rent or mortgage and what utility bills are costing each month. If a customer is currently renter, introduce tax write-offs available for homeowners. You may also play to the overall improvement in lifestyle when one owns a home. If a customer owns an older home, you can use these questions to lead into a presentation about the savings a new home will provide. There are many directions you can take the conversation depending on the customers wants and current situation.

Beyond asking questions, one of the keys to unveiling and magnifying urgency is siting the customer. The more you take customers out and show them home sites, the more contracts you will write. Siting is the first and foremost way to get customers to see, touch and experience the possibility of owning one of your homes. Recognize as you site that some homes may not be the right fit. You may need to show customers several homes to find the perfect one for them. Ideally, the available homes you have are different in distinct aspects like floor plan configuration, lot location, elevation, designer features and the like. Demonstrate how each home is unlike any other. You never know what one special characteristic will make the difference for a customer— whether it be the way the house is facing, the exterior color, the floor plan, proximity to amenities or a variety of other features.

A great way to discern what special features may play to a customer's interest is to identify his or her personality type. When it comes to tipping customers over in the buying process and magnifying urgency, playing to personality types is a really effective approach. Knowing how each personality type operates, and being able to identify a personality type when you meet a customer, will allow you to extend unparalleled customer service that will absolutely make a difference at the end of the day. It's really important to help customers in the ways in which they need to be helped. Recognizing what a customer needs and interacting with them in ways that they find relatable will undoubtedly magnify a customer's urgency and enhance the willingness to buy.

Once you see your customer display willingness, ask him or her to buy. Asking customers to buy, and doing so more than once, builds urgency. Although customers create their own urgency, you are the impetus for urgency in many ways. Urgency is excitement and passion— and it's a feeling that you will transfer your customers.

### Need to Think About it

"*I need to think about it*" is the all-time fallback for customers who want to delay making a decision. In knowing that if a customer has come to you, he or she has come for a reason, also know not to take "*I need to think about it*" at face value. That is not to say you shouldn't honor when a customer gives that response, but you should certainly be prepared to go further with the customer if that's what he or she needs. More often then not, when a customer says, "*I need to think about it,*" the translation is, "*There's something I'm still unsure of.*" In most cases, if a customer doesn't like your homes, you'll be aware of it and there's really nothing you can do to change it. But if you know customers like what they see, this response is a smokescreen for something else. Oftentimes, they are holding back and not telling you their real reasons for hesitating.

Though you may feel like you've exhausted everything you have to offer, do not cave in when a customer expresses the need to think about things more. Don't give up, don't resist, don't give in. There's clearly something else the customer needs that he or she hasn't heard yet, or there is something the customer hasn't told you yet that supplies a real reason for holding back.

Whatever the reason, there is something going on that is making the customer uncomfortable about moving forward. At such a juncture, you really need to step in and be empathetic with people as to try and figure it out. This is a great opportunity for you to isolate a customer's objection as means to providing a solution. A great question to ask in this situation is, "*Other than needing to think about it what additional concerns do you* have?" remember, it's okay to dare to dig. So kindly ask, *"If you don't mind me asking, what more do you need to think about?"* This level of open, honest communication permissions them to be open and honest with you, especially if they sense that you are coming from a place of really wanting to help them if you can. It's another example of how you can lead the dance, lead the interaction, and possibly lead them to buy now.

Customers will generally share the easy answers first. The easy answers are things that don't make them "look bad" in the minds of others. But it's the harder truths that you want to get at because this is where you can really help. They generally won't open up to share more difficult reasons until they have a real sense that you care and are truly there to help. Dig deep to find out. *"What are your concerns? What else?"* Sometimes—particularly in a tough economy—people have a difficult time talking about what's going on in their lives.

Listen well and quietly be empathetic as customers divulge more personal information. That means the customer trusts you enough to open up, and so it's important for you to return the sentiment. If nothing else has worked in the way of siting, questioning and providing third-party endorsements, try sharing a story about another buyer who had a similar experience and how they prevailed. Remember that you are not there just to sell a house; you're there to help a customer purchase a home and to help them figure out how to put the pieces together to do so.[*]

## Recap

• First, recognize that each customer comes to you for a reason. Though individuals may profess objections to buying a new home, there is something that brought each one of them to you. Find out customers'

---

[*] If you encounter an objection or concern in your marketplace that I do not address here, please call me with questions at (916) 768-5525. There is no cost to you.

reasons and uncover and identify their roadblocks so you can help them make forward progress.

• Isolate issues so you can gain clarity on an objection and be better equipped to help a customer work through it.

• Employ effective techniques depending on what type of obstacle you have encountered to help provide your customer with a solution.

• Ask questions and listen intently and openly to what a customer says— and doesn't say. Also be willing to reach customers on a personal level and dig deep to get results.

**Crucial Questions**

- *"If you don't mind me asking, what's holding you back?"*

Credit Issues
- *"Do you plan on financing the home?"*
- *"Have you talked to a lender yet?"*
- *"How much did they say you could quality for?" "How's your credit? Do you know your FICO score?"*
- *"Have you ever owned a home before?"*
- *"Do you own now or are you currently renting?"*
- *"Have you had a bankruptcy, foreclosure or short sale within the last two years?"*
- *"Have you had any late payments of more than 30 days in the last two years?"*
- *"Have you considered working with a credit professional?"*

No Down payment
- *"How much do you have saved for a down payment and closing costs?"*
- *"Where is your down payment coming from? Do you have access to any gift funds?"*

- *"How do you feel about dipping into your 401k to invest in your new home?"*
- *"Did you know you can adjust your tax withholdings and bring home more money each month?"*
- *"How much can you save each month toward a down payment?"*
- *"Are you willing to do what it takes to make this home yours?"*

Get a Better Deal

- *"What other homes are you seriously considering?*
- *"What was lacking that you didn't purchase it?"*
- *"Of all the homes you've seen, how do ours compare?"*
- *"If you get a great deal on this, would you buy it today?"*
- *"If the company is willing to make you a deal, how much are you willing to give us in the way of a deposit?"*

Market Timing and Price Decline

- *"What do you think about the market?*
- *"How do you think it compares to three to five years ago?"*
- *"What do you think about today's prices?*
- *"Have you seen how low interest rates are?"*
- *"Do you believe that now might be the time to buy?"*
- *"What's your timeline for buying? "What's it based on?"*
- *"If you found the perfect house today, when would you buy it?"*
- *What are you waiting for?"*

Need to Think About It

- *"Other than needing to think about it, what additional concerns do you have?"*
- *"If you don't mind me asking, what more do you need to think about?"*
- *"What are your concerns? What else?"*

# MASTERING THE CLOSE

*"If you want to double your success rate, double your failure rate."*
— Michael Eisner

Though every single part of the home-buying experience you create is a step toward achieving your sales goals, the final, final close is the number one most important question during your presentation. In large part this is because the close is embedded in every part of your presentation, in every single question leading up to that critical decision-making moment when you ask the customer to buy. Asking for the sale, also uncovers any objections and concerns that may be holding the customer back from purchasing right away.

## Habits of a Master Closer

The first rule of thumb is to always be closing. What this means is to continually ask questions that help you understand your customer's perspective and guide his or her thinking toward moving forward with the purchase today. Always closing is a superbly effective sales technique because as you do so, you tailor your presentation to the customers' interests and automatically builds up to the final, final close with the customer's steady participation. Strive to close on the purchase agreement during the first visit.

*The Theory of Space*

The Theory of Space describes how the qualities in which you stand permissions others to be the same. Throughout the presentation you are adjust your behaviors to mirror the characteristics of your customer. Then, there are times when you have to step into the behaviors that you want them to share with you. There is an empathetic art to this line of reasoning. As you ask your customer the final closing question, you must stand in a space of positivity. Be bold and confident as you ask them if they want to buy. As you stand in a self-assured *"Yes"* and emit that courageously positive quality, your customer can likewise step into *"Yes"* mode with you.

*Look them in the Eyes*

To help prompt a positive outcome, there are four seemingly small but magnificently significant gestures you can make when you're asking for the sale that will support your customers in moving forward immediately. The first is to look them in the eyes as you ask. Good eye contact demonstrates your trustworthiness, sincerity and confidence. As the customer pickups on your strengths, it helps them have the courage to make the decision to buy today.

*What's in a Name? POWER!*

Second, always use the customer's name when asking for the sale. This is an area where the 100% rule again applies. Use your customer's name 100 percent of the time. *"So, name, what do you think about moving forward with the purchase agreement today?"*

There is a lot of power in using the customer's name throughout your presentation but especially when asking the closing question. Using the customer's name as you ask helps the customer feel a more personal connection to you and the home they are considering buying.

## Be a Bobble Head

A third habit to cultivate is to subtly nod your head "Yes" as you ask your closing question. Though it is less direct than saying someone's name or looking someone in the eyes, the subconscious effect is compelling. Body language speaks volumes in personal interactions. It's the unspoken way to lead the customer. As you stand in the physical space of "yes", likewise, your customer may follow your lead and answer with and "okay".

They may also ask a question. They may express an concern. They may give you excuses as to why they can't buy. They may tell you that they need to think about it. No matter what they express and say...do the following.

## Shut Up

Finally, when you do ask a final, final closing question, do not say another word. Wait to speak again, as long as necessary, for the customer to respond. And, give them the conversational space to answer with as much information as they are willing to share. If the silent pause is uncomfortable for you, notice your discomfort and breathe! Remember, as you ask questions you are guiding the customer toward the feelings of having a new home now. Allow the space and time for customers to experience their feelings and for them to share them with you. The pause also gives you the opportunity to observe and look for any queues as to what else you may need to do or say to support the customer. Be quiet, look and listen of the most important behaviors to practice after the close for the sale. Make a point to get absolutely comfortable with the silence.

## ASK More than Once

As you ask questions throughout your sales presentation—always closing the customer—establish a second context for yourself: Ask for the sale at least three times, in three different ways. You ask for the sale more than once, making adjustments as you go, because it can take time for customers to build interest and allow themselves to become interested.

Asking them for the sale tempts them to buy and, the bottom line is, unless and until you ask customers if they'd like to move forward today, they're not as tempted. They need to be tempted to buy. Lead them to temptation. When you ask—especially more than once—you're demonstrating you are ready and willing to move forward, which gives them the ability to step into their own willingness to move forward. Play off of that human interconnectedness.

Enact these five habits in the process of always closing. Welcome your customer into *"Yes"* mode with you, look your customer in the eye, use your customer's name and, nod your head, allow for a pause after you ask your closing question, and ask more than once. In doing so, you are helping your customer build the comfort he or she needs to make an affirmative decision. You are influencing in meaningful and effective ways the opportunity for your customer to own one of your homes—to make a better life by moving forward today.


## Adjust to the Customer

As the linchpin of your sales presentation, the final, final close requires different approaches depending on your buyer's character and the circumstances surrounding the purchase.

Leading up to the final close, you should already have a clear understanding of what your customers want and need—their situation and problems, and the implications of their problems. This includes where they live now, why they are moving, and how their current situation is adversely affecting their lives on a mental, emotional, financial, or relationship level. You should have sited each customer and narrowed the selection to the best site for his or her preferences, and you should have also already spoken about the down payment and financing. Knowing where customers stand in life is vital to you helping them move forward, just like understanding each person's personality type.

The expression "opposites attract" doesn't apply in sales and especially not in new home sales. People tend to buy from people they like and people tend to like those who are like themselves. The most effective frontline Sales PROfessionals behave as a chameleon and adjust to customers. You want to treat customers the way they want and need to be treated, and sell customers the way they like to be sold. To do so, make sure you know the telltale signs of the four personality types: controller, analyst, promoter, and supporter. Just as a customer's personality type tells you how to give your presentation, it will reveal to you the best closes to use.

## 12 Techniques for Closing the Sale

Each personality type possesses distinct qualities and characteristics that can make it easier or more difficult to close. The key is to know how to use these traits to your advantage. Following are twelve techniques, including talking points and interaction tips, to help you close the different buyer types so you can effectively close for the sale today.

### *Controllers*

Controllers are doers. They are results-driven, business-first people. They are direct and decisive, and can even be impatient. They have a need to be right, or at least to think they're right about things, so be prepared for controllers to tell you everything they want right when they walk in the door. You want to be to the point as you work with this group. Controllers will respect you for that, especially when you ask them to buy.

### Direct Close

While one predominant school of thought in sales is not to ask a yes-or-no question, such an approach falls well in-line with normal communication. It is acceptable to ask a yes-or-no question, especially with controllers. They are very direct people and will have no problem with a straightforward question: *"Is this the home you want to own?"* By the time you're making your final close, the controller has most likely made up his or her mind. If you receive a *"Yes,"* to the last question, move on with *"What do you think about moving forward with the purchase agreement today?"* If you receive a *"No,"* ask another direct and simple question: *"OK, how come?"* or *"Why not?"*

There may be an objection you can overcome in order to turn the situation around, so from there you want to try and work with whatever prompted the *"No."*

Handshake Close

With the very direct controllers, it's important to not just engage them directly in return, but to be assertive with them. When your presentation is complete and you're looking to close the controller, extend your hand to them, just like you did upon your introduction. This is a strong assertion that you're ready to seal the deal with them on their new home. Look the controller right in the eyes, nod your head, and say, *"So, [Customer Name], do we have a deal?"* or *"Are you ready to move forward today, [Customer Name]?"* You can even offer your handshake in a congratulatory spirit: *"Congratulations. It sounds like we have a deal?"*

Takeaway Close

If and when your first two attempts don't work in eliciting an affirmative response, try a takeaway close. The takeaway close can be an extremely effective technique with people who are controllers, but it requires you to be confident. You're challenging the controller, in a sense, and the controller tends to be dominant. In this instance, you want to magnify the controller's urgency and need to call his or her own shots in life: *"You know, it only takes one lucky buyer to purchase this house—and it is the best one. Do you want to make it yours before someone else does, name?"* Controllers don't like the thought or feeling of losing control over their own destiny. You may also tell them about another set of customers who are also interested in the same homesite. Ask them, *"If they decide to buy it, which homesite would be your second choice?"* Controllers also tend to not to like to settle for second best. This line of reasoning may propel them to move forward immediately.

## Analysts

Analysts are thinkers. They tend to be more thoughtful, detail-oriented people. They typically want all the information before they make a decision and are very persistent as they gather their information. Likewise, you need to be persistent with them by asking them to move forward at least three times.

They tend to be slower to make buying decisions, so it's important to appeal to their logic and their intellect when asking for the sale. Analysts tend to have a need to not be wrong about their decision, therefore be thorough and evincing in your approach to analysts.

## Logical Close

With analytical people, comparison or value-driven closes often resonate the most. Chances are, they will know the market trends and the finer points of your competition as well as you do—down to the features, benefits, and warranties—so you really have to know information forwards and backwards to connect well with this group. Ask questions that allow you to gauge what an analyst is thinking. Gain agreement as you appeal to their thinking faculties. *"We've gone through all your needs and the home meets your needs well, right?"* *"So name, don't you think it makes sense to move forward with the purchase agreement today?"* Engage analysts on a cerebral basis as you ask for the sale.

## Reduce to Ridiculous Close

Because analysts are so value-driven, they will be interested in how the numbers break down. Reducing to the ridiculous is a great technique to employ with analysts because you can reduce the amount they're spending to a per-month, weekly or per-day amount. For example, an additional $1,000 in a purchase price only accounts for about $5 more per month, $1.25 per week which is 16¢ a day. When you point that out to an analyst, it will resonate. It's a great way to justify value to analysts and, once you've shown them how little something costs, you can follow up with, "*Based on the comparison, would you agree that ours is the best value?*" Now, ask again: "*So, does it make sense, name, to do the paperwork?*"

## Additional Info Close

Analysts put a lot of time and energy into ensuring no mistake is made. As you close them, honor their need for information with a simple question such as, "*What additional information do you need, [Customer Name], to formulate a decision?*" or "*What else are you still wondering about, [Customer Name]?*" If you feel comfortable being more assertive, ask, "*Is there anything else you're still wondering about before we do the paperwork, [Customer Name]?*"

## *Promoters*

Promoters are talkers. They place a lot of emphasis on personal relationships and have a lot of friends. As super social beings, they tend to be expressive, dramatic, enthusiastic, fun, and emotional. Their they brains comprehend many things at once, so they sometimes come across as lacking focus. Therefore, you need to keep your presentation moving, ready to change direction on the fly, especially when you notice them losing interest in what you are showing or saying. They also tend to be spontaneous decision-makers. So when you ask the promoter to buy today engage them in the excitement of the experience through your words and actions.

## Assumptive Close

As long as you are positive and ready to move ahead, the promoter will likely follow. This is the sure-fire group with which to assume the sale. Act as if the customer has already made the decision and turn the focus of the conversation to their options or dates, or something else that implies the house is theirs: *"Will a September completion date work for you?"* Assuming permission to move ahead is a great technique to use with the promoter. They will enthusiastically hop on your surfboard and ride the wave of excitement all the way to the close with you, if you take them there.

*Are you ready to take this off the market today?*

## Realm of Possibility Close

You always want to be forward-looking with the promoter. This group often thinks about the bigger, better possibilities. Play on their excitement: *"Aren't you excited, [Customer Name], to be getting a brand new beautiful home today?"* If it seems as though the purchase is going to be a push—with credit issues, a current lease or some other consideration slowing down the process or making it more difficult to buy—ask the customer, *"Are you willing to do what it takes to make this happen today?"* Being emotional people, promoters' feelings will play a big role in their decision-making. Ask the promoter, *"How do you feel about making this one yours today, [Customer Name]?"*

## Concession Close

And finally, once you've attempted the other two closes and addressed any of their objections and concerns, try increasing the excitement with a giveaway. Promoters are big on perks. Anything you can do to make the purchase more tempting is sure to get their attention.

Find out what you might offer to further entice the customer to buy today by asking, *"What do you plan on purchasing for your home after you move in?"* That way you'll know if your builder offers an option that your customer may need, such as ceiling fans, a garage door opener, concrete work, window coverings, landscaping or appliances just to name a few. In incentivizing the close, however, you don't want to offer the extras right up front. The minute you offer it, it becomes a given. Instead, use them as a temptation tool. *"If I could get you the kitchen appliances, name, would you buy today?"*

Or if the customer asks for $5,000 off the price, come back at them with, *"If my builder gives you $5,000 off the price, when would you buy it?"* The customer will know the right answer is *"Today."* Use the concession as a bargaining chip. Trade the promoter for a buying decision today, and perhaps also solidify the agreement with a higher deposit. Don't begin to negotiate unless the customer is willing to move forward right away. Including options, such as appliances or anything they may need to purchase after close of escrow is a great way to lead promoters to "yes".

*Supporters*

Supporters are listeners. They tend to be very friendly and relationship-oriented, though not as expressive as the promoter. They tend to depend upon approval from others, desiring to please others above themselves. Empathy is extremely important in working with supporters. Because the relationship is the absolute most important with this group, you may permit yourself to give more space on asking for the close than with the other groups. Supporters do not respond well to pressure. You have to be patient, as they can be slow to make a decision, and take a service-oriented approach. Your primary effort in closing the supporter should be to reaffirm that moving forward with the home is the right decision. In fact, the supporter will oftentimes defer to someone else to make the decision. That person can be you!

Trial Close

Trial closes allow you to match the more subtle personality of the supporter. They are typically in the form of *"What if...?"* statements—somewhat hypothetical in nature. *"If you owned the home, which room would you make your office?"* and *"Would your furniture work in here?"* This way you can test the emotional waters and get a feeling as to what they are feeling.

Or, to appeal even more to the supporters' home- and family-centered sentiments, *"If you purchase the home, will the holidays be at your house this year?"* Committing to making a decision can scare this group, so it's best to ease them into the purchase by really being supportive and affirming.

Emotional Close

Supporters are emotional people. Connecting their sense of ownership to something they feel strongly about is an effective approach. *"Wouldn't it be nice to make this a home for your family?"* As you seek to be empathetic, let them know that you are really there for them. *"This is the right home for you, and I'll be there for you every step of the way, okay?"* Deliver that wonderful, unparalleled service so supporters can feel assured in their decision. *"How would you feel, name, about completing the purchase agreement with me today?"* Make it personal by putting yourself into the closing experience with them so they feel completely supported by you.

## Tell them to Buy, Nicely

Contrary to how most may think, you can tell the customer to buy. Making the decision for supporters is the most supportive way you can help them move forward. This is not to be confused with ordering the customer to buy. Remember, people who tend to be more supportive in nature will often defer to others to make decisions.

Provided that you have truly established a relationship of trust with this customer to the point that he or she regards you not just as *a* trusted advisor but *the* trusted advisor, you will be empowered to give the OK sign. This is an artful act of making a decision for a customer and balancing it so as not to come across as pushy. Lower your voice, perhaps casually positioned standing in the kitchen or seated on the furniture in your model, then simply say, *"Here, [Customer Name], let me help you. This is where you sign."* This is one of the boldest closes you can make. It should be done with the utmost of care and light heartedness. Remember, the Theory of Space dictates that the qualities in which you stand permission others to do the same. Often times the supporter is afraid of moving forward, especially alone. If you are truly there for them, you can be the one with the courage to support them in being courageous too. Now that's customer service for one of the most challenging buyers!

## Unlimited Possibility

It is your beingness—what you do and the actions you take—that will get you what you want in life. Mastering the close is a matter of cultivating your own state of being, as well as your ability to adapt to others' states of being. Each time you set the context for a positive buying experience, carefully tending to the unique customer in front of you, you are establishing the possibility for success. The close is where you seize the opportunity, where you make that success real.

## Recap

The habits of a master closer include looking the customer in the eyes when you ask the final, final close, nodding your head "yes", always using their name when asking and listening to their full and complete response.

• There are four different personality types for you to be prepared to work with: Controller, Analyst, Promoter, and Supporter (CAPS).

• With each buyer type, ask for the sale at least three times in three different ways—paying special attention to which methods are the most effective for each group.

Mike Eisner said at the onset of this chapter that *"If you want to double your success rate, double your failure rate."* I want to suggest that if you are committed to increasing your closing ratio, especially on the first visit, double, triple or even quadruple your asking for the sale rate.[*]

## Crucial Questions

Controller
• *"What do you think about moving forward with the purchase agreement today?"*
• *"Is this the home you want to own?*
• *"Do we have a deal?*
• *"Are you ready to move forward today?"*
• *"Do you want to make this your home before anyone else does?"*

---

[*] If you would like to practice closing with me, please call (916) 768-5525. There is no cost to you.

Analyst
- *"Of all the homes that you've seen so far, how do ours compare?"*
- *"What other homes are you seriously considering?"*
- *"Based on a comparison, would you agree that ours is the best value?"*
- *"Does it make sense to do the paperwork?"*
- *"What additional information do you need to make a decision?"*
- *"Is there anything else you're still wondering about before we do the paperwork?"*

Promoter
- *"Aren't you excited to be getting a brand new beautiful house today?"*
- *"Are you willing to do what it takes to make this happen today?"*
- *"How do you feel about making this one yours today?"*
- *"What do you plan on purchasing for your home after you move in?"*
- *"If I could get you the kitchen appliances, would you buy today?"*
- *"If my builder gives you $5,000 off the price, when would you buy it?"*

Supporter
- *"If you owned the home which room would be your office?*
- *Would your furniture work in here?"*
- *"If you purchase the home, will the holidays be at your house this year?"*
- *"Wouldn't it be nice to make this a home for your family?"*
- *"How do you feel, <u>name</u>, about completing the purchase agreement with me today?"*

# FANTASTIC FOLLOW-UP

*"We are what we repeatedly do. Excellence then is not an act, but a habit."*

– Aristotle

****

*When I was the Vice President of Sales and Marketing for Beazer homes, I used to make rounds visiting all of my communities, especially when big promotions were happening. During one major promotion, I stopped in a community to check in with one of my best salespeople. It was about 8 p.m. when I got to her sales center—that's how busy things were—and I remember her looking at me, distraught with concern. She said, "Christine, I did not sell a single home today. I don't know what happened." Then she showed me a stack of completed visitor surveys.*

*I walked over to her telephone, pretended to dial a number and conducted a mock follow-up call. When I hung up I said, "What I'd like for you to do is make all these calls before you leave for the day and see if you can schedule times to get people back in tomorrow." About an hour later, I got a call from her as she was driving home. She had scheduled three appointments for the following day.*

*By following up with the customers while the experience was fresh in their minds, she demonstrated unparalleled presale customer service and was able to capitalize on the momentum she had created earlier in the day to retain the interest of her customers which resulted in sales.*

****

## Why Follow Up?

The number one reason to follow up with your customers is that calls lead to contacts, and contacts lead to contracts. Following up with customers is a simple way to create tipping points in your sales success. A brief phone call, followed up by a short email or text, demonstrates to customers that you are at their service even after they've left your sales center. Follow-up is one of the foremost opportunities to demonstrate the quality of your company, and to garner results in the process. The more contacts you have with your prospects early on in their experience, the more sales you make faster.

## How to Follow Up?

Though many people prefer the convenience of email, the absolute best way to make contact with your customers is to speak with them. This is also the best way to connect with them. For starters, it's likely that your competition isn't making personal phone calls, which means that you doing so will set you apart from the rest. By making the effort to personally reach your customers, you will show your dedication in helping them move forward in their own lives. Moreover, phone calls and text messages are far and away more effective than emails. Though email is easy and seems non-intrusive, they also are easily deleted. When it comes to reaching your customers, always pick up the phone and call first. Then send a text message. This will make a huge difference in your effectiveness and response rate.

### *Tricks of the Trade*

To ensure you have everything you need to reach your customers and provide them with the best possible service, verify your customers contact information before they leave your sales center. Because calling will be your primary mode for reaching them, first make sure you've got the correct phone number. It is important to realize that not all customers will provide accurate information. Most will, but there is the occasional person who doesn't want to be reached for one reason or another. So, to account for any inaccurate information, there's a simple trick of the trade.

When a customer gives you his or her phone number, repeat the number back them. But, invert two of the numbers while doing so. For example, if you are given a number with the last four digits -5525, say something like, *"Ok, let me make sure I got this right. 916-768-5255?"* If the customer corrects you, it confirms you were given the right phone number. If the customer doesn't correct you, chances are the number is a fake and that customer isn't someone you want to spend time pursuing.

If a customer hands you back the visitor survey and you notice he or she has completed everything but omitted a phone number, simply ask for it. *"I noticed you didn't include your phone number. Would you mind if I followed up with you by phone?"* or *"Would it be okay if I followed up with you?"*

If you've truly demonstrated unparalleled customer service—taking the time to learn about an individual's situation and any personal problems, and the implications of those problems; demonstrating the value and quality of your homes; and discussing financing and the options available—most people will provide you with a legitimate phone number on second thought. If a customer responds with something along the lines of *"Well, I'd rather not give it out."* Then simply ask again, *"Are you sure you don't want me to follow up with you?"* Don't push the issue too much if a customer seems resistant, but most people will include the phone number upon you asking a second time.

In addition to phone numbers, verify personal email addresses using the same approach. Having accurate contact information is critical for effective follow-up.


## When to Follow Up?

Same day follow up is most effective for scheduling return appointments. Habitually, make your calls and send text and email messages at the end of each day. If your don't have any customers, spend your final 30-60 minutes making follow-up calls as a last order of business before closing your models. Not only will you feel accomplished in the service you provided all day, you may even set up some customer appointments. If you don't make follow-up calls at the end of the business day, you can be assured you won't get any next-day return appointments. Conversely, if you do make your follow-up calls right away, you are pretty much guaranteed to schedule some return appointments.

Likewise, make it a habit to make additional follow up calls first thing in the morning to those you didn't reach the previous evening. Arrive at your office early to get your models open and ready for business. Then take 30-60 minutes at the start of your day to sit down and make your calls. Making your calls in the morning can be a great way to get in the sales groove for the day.

Though you can certainly work follow-up calls in during the day if you have the opportunity, you want to be sure to dedicate a specific time to the process. Making a habit of follow-up is one of the keys to generating results. Whichever time of day you find the most effective for making your follow-up calls, integrate it into your daily routine.

*Data Entry*

Data entry is one of the biggest obstacles when it comes to follow-up in new home sales. With regard to the importance of follow-up, it must be said that continuing contact with customers is not possible if you don't input the data to begin with. For most people, data entry is a painful part of the process. But it has to be done.

Ideally, you would input information in the computer database as soon as the customer leaves your sales center. Also, put the customer's name and cell phone number in your cell phone. Taking a few minutes after each customer breaks up the process for you, but it also allows the company to capitalize on its automated email campaigns.

The sooner you get customer information in the system, the sooner your company and your customer benefit from the contact that was made. Figure out what works for you and make data entry a part of your routine, just like the follow-up itself. The benefits far outweigh the burden.

## Three Phases of Follow-up

When it comes to the creating a wonderful home-buying experience, there are three phases during which you want to follow up with your customers: after the initial visit, after the purchase agreement is completed, and after move-in day. The first phase occurs with your future customers, your prospective homebuyers, with whom you're following up after presenting your models. In the second phase, you are following up with your customers who have completed the purchase agreement and are currently in escrow. And for the third phase, you are following up with your customers who have closed escrow and are moved into their new home.

Future customers are the primary focus of follow-up efforts, as they are the ones who you need to capture and who may require more persistent effort. However, as a New Home Sales PROfessional, it is your job to tend to every single customer across all phases of the home-buying process to ensure a positive and powerful experience for them. These three home-buying phases and tips will help you engage with customers at each juncture.

### After the Visit

When a customer comes in for an initial visit, you want to of course have him or her complete the visitor survey so you can capture and verify contact information. After the customer has left, be prepared to reach out that same day.

## Same-day Follow-up

Same-day follow-up is incredibly effective because you will both be fresh on each other's minds. You'll remember the personal details—and hopefully have recorded some notes—that will make a difference in extending personalized service, and the customer will be able to more readily recall the benefits and features of your homes.

You may hesitate to follow up on the same day as a customer's visit for fear that it seems pushy, to which there is some simple advice: if you don't act pushy, you won't be perceived as pushy. Approach it in the spirit of being attentive and helpful.

Same-day follow-up will automatically differentiate you from other builders in the industry. At the earliest, most companies call a day later, or more likely a week later. But by then, customers have forgotten what your homes look like because they've been out viewing other communities. One challenge in the new home industry is that there are very few model complexes that stand completely apart. But if you pick up the phone and dial customers, they will remember you and your homes and they will recognize the service your builder provides.

## Script

When you reach out to customers for your same-day follow-up, there is a simple script you can use to demonstrate your customer service. It will also help you find out where you and your homes stand in the mind of the customer.

*"Hi [Customer Name], this is [Your Name] from [Company Name]. I just wanted to touch base with you before I left for the evening to see what you're thinking and feeling about the home, and if you have any additional questions that I can answer for you?"*

Approaching your customers this way on the same day as their visit also gives you the ability to answer any questions they may have thought of after leaving. Customers often get caught up in the experience of touring homes. It is only when the pressure subsides that they think of more questions. Following up the same day also allows you to overcome any objections the customers may have. Some may really want to buy but have specific concerns they aren't sure can be met. Same-day follow-up calls enable you to immediately answer with customers' questions and capitalize on their urgency.

Above all else, though, the primary objective of the same-day follow-up call is to schedule a day and time for a customer to return. Of course you call the customer to continue demonstrating the quality service, to answer questions, and to overcome objections—but ultimately you call the customer to get him or her back in the sales center to move forward with the purchase.

If you are unable to schedule a return appointment, keep at it by asking: *"Would it be okay if I followed up with you the day after tomorrow? Or in a week?"* Try to gain agreement from the customer about when to speak again. You may also ask, *"When should I follow-up with you again?"* Then follow through on the day exactly as they suggested.

## Dials vs. Conversations

Follow-up calls are not about dialing numbers, they are about actually reaching people. Each follow-up call should result in a conversation with the customer that allows you to build upon the relationship and continue to advance the sale.

When you sit down at the end of the day to make your follow-up calls, attempt at least three times to reach your customers. If you get a voicemail, hang up and go to your next contact on the list. Once you make it through your list, start back up at the top and try again.

On your third attempt, leave a message using the script above along with your phone number and email address. After three attempts, most people recognize that someone is sincerely trying to get ahold of them.

Their curiosity will kick in and they will answer. Don't give up. You want to be always, continually advancing the sale forward.

## Follow-up Email

Phone call follow-up should always take the first priority, but emails can also be an effective measure. When it comes to your follow-up email, you need a catchy subject line that is no longer than a few words.

The email message should be short and sweet—a few sentences at most with a call to action right at the beginning: "*Hey [Customer Name], let's schedule a time for you to come back in.*" Within the body of your email, consider any links or widgets that will entice the customer to continue looking into your homes on his or her own. Also highlight any key phrases in red text or a similar color. Make sure that important information jumps out at readers. To conclude the email, let your customer know you will be following up with them soon: "*I will touch base with you again on Saturday.*" or "*I will call you again in a week.*" And just as with the phone call, do exactly as you promise.

## Realtor Follow-up

In addition to your customers, you also want to reach out to their realtors directly. Not only may realtors help you get in touch with your customers, they also are people with whom you can build long-lasting relationships.

## Repeat and End

Follow up with your customers until you have left three messages. At that point make your last attempt. Here's a suggested script:

*"Hi [Customer Name], It's [Your Name] with [Company Name]. I just wanted to touch base with you one more time. I've left you three messages and haven't heard back from you. I'm wondering if you are still considering our homes and if you'd like me to continue to follow up with you? Please give me a quick call back at [Your phone number] or shoot me a quick email at [Your Email}. I want to let you know that I'm here to help you when the time is right for you. Have a great day!"*

If you still don't get an answer or hear back, you should be prepared to wrap up contact with that customer. Your focus should remain on those customers who are more urgent in their search for a home and more likely to buy. At that point, allow the company standard email campaign take over.

## Text Messages and the Handwritten Note

Contrary to popular suggestions these days, the handwritten note as part of presale follow-up for all prospects is, overall, a waste of time and money. While it is admittedly a nice gesture, and can be effective for builder communities where there is little traffic, handwritten notes are rarely so persuasive as to tip the customer over into scheduling a return visit, let alone purchasing a home. These days, a text message is way more likely to get you a response. First, text messages are short and to the point. They are a way of maintaining contact with your prospects without overpowering or being too assertive. You get the speed of a phone call and the safe distance of an email. And you are much more likely to get a response because it is easy for the customer to respond to. Save the handwritten thank-you note for those who actually purchase.

## After the Purchase

For customers who have completed the purchase agreement, set a goal of earning referrals while they're still in escrow. To do so, play on customers' anticipatory frame of mind—you want to work the angle of their excitement.

*"Hi [Customer Name], This is [Your Name] from [Company Name]. I wanted to congratulate you for purchasing your home. You made a great decision! Do you have any questions that I can answer for you before I leave for the day?"*

Continue to extend the level of customer service your customers have gotten used to from you and your company. Be constantly there for your customers. Additionally, when you make the congratulations call, seize the opportunity to tell the customer about your company's referral program: *"I'm also calling to remind you about our awesome homebuyer referral program."*

As an added perk after customers decide to purchase a home from you, send them something personal. This is the opportunity to take a few minutes to write a thank-you note expressing your gratitude for their business. Customers will appreciate the act. When you send the note, also include a few business cards that your customer can pass onto others.

*After the Move*

When your customer has the keys to his or her very own house, excitement is peaked—take the opportunity to honor the experience. Call right away: *"Hi, it's [Your Name], Just wanted to touch base with you and see how you are doing in your new home and if there's anything I can do to help?"* Also take the opportunity to make a personal visit to the house and extend a gift. Give something, such as a plant, that will be long lasting and create a memory in your customer's mind. At the very least, your customer will appreciate the opportunity to show off the new home. And, as you fulfill your customer service promise, you also want to ask about future clients to serve: *"Have you come across anyone who would be interested in living here too?"* When you create fans in your customers, you can build a following among others.

## All-in Follow-up

In many ways, following up is the culmination of everything else you do as an exceptional New Home Sales PROfessional. Following up takes the committed mindset of a moneymaker. It takes knowing your why. It's part of bringing in the business. It is most certainly an exercise in being a master communicator. It's about knowing how to connect different personalities. It's about continuing the perfect demonstration even beyond the model homes and sales center. Following up, if done right and right away, is a great way to stomp the competition. It's also a great way to keep track of where you stand with contingencies. It's a prime method for helping customers overcome their objections once they leave your sales center to think things over. And it is the way to win the sale.

As you conduct your FAN-tastic follow-up, recognize that it is an opportunity for you to put everything else into practice, to capitalize on your hard work, to achieve your goals. At the end of the day, you aren't just following up with your customers—you're following up with your own wants and needs, your own dreams.

## Recap

• Follow-up doesn't have to be overwhelming to be effective. Simply make a habit of doing it. Moreover, following up with your customers—especially via phone calls—can create a tipping point in your sales.

## Crucial Questions

• *"Would you mind if I followed up with you?"*
• *Do you have any additional questions that I can answer for you?"*
• *"Would it be OK if I followed up with you the day after tomorrow, or in a week?"*
• *"When should I follow up with you again?"*
• *"Is there anything I can do to help?"*
• *"Have you come across anyone who would be interested in living here too?"*

# AFTERWORD: COMING FULL CIRCLE

*"Every action generates a force of energy that comes back to us in like kind."*

– Deepak Chopra

## Karma

On a metaphysical level, spiritual laws govern success in new home sales. Karma is the understanding and the realization that as you put out good energy, you get good energy back. You get good things back. Therefore, it's important to choose actions that generate happiness and success and wealth for others if that's what you want to come back to you. Everything that you say and do, regardless of how seemingly insignificant, affects your family, the community and all human beings for as long as you live.

To illustrate, one of the things that profoundly influenced me over thirty years ago happened at my very first sales job right out of high school. I was a young girl working the Sunrise shopping mall in Citrus Heights, California for a company called Swiss Colony. Working there, I was taught a six-step selling process and had hourly sales goals. The man who owned the franchise was football coach and one of the things that he taught me, over thirty years ago, was to *"Do your 100 percent best job with every customer always, every time, without fail."* Here it is over three decades later, and I've made his edict part of my business practices and teachings ever since. I call it my 100% rule.

Hold yourself and your sales people to that standard. Can you let one customer slide through your sale centers without greeting them properly, without finding out their situation, without assessing their needs well and taking the time to demonstrate our models, without showing the customer the value and the quality the builder puts into our homes? I am still sending out and echoing his message that he gave to me years ago, and others I have influenced send the ripples and echoes out also. That's how it works. This is how what you say and do—and sometimes it seems so little—can have a tremendous effect in the bigger picture of our lives.

Everything comes back to you, in one way or another, whether it's directly or indirectly. It can be really obvious and almost immediate when direct or there may be a delay and be less obvious when indirect. You don't necessarily experience the results of Karma until years later. For example, after high school I applied to be an exchange student and, to make a long story short, ended up being accepted to go to Brazil but, through an inexplicable set of circumstances, the opportunity was taken away from me. In the meantime, the exchange program kept sending me all the information for me to take this trip to Brazil to do a year-long exchange. I kept receiving information from the program and I figured it was just an error. But ultimately I received a letter from my host family welcoming me to their home. I really wanted to go. I had worked hard. I saved my money. I had applied to the program twice. Other family members were pitching in funds to send me. It was my dream. So I sent the Brazilian family a letter and asked them if I could come anyway, even though the official sponsors had for some reason changed their mind. I figured that if the host family wanted me with the program, they would want me without the program. But, in the meantime, they were sent another girl. So, they told their friends about me and their friends invited me to live in their home for a year. That was thirty something years ago and I have stayed very close to my Brazilian families over the years. We are connected for life.

Fast forward to seven years ago. My Brazilian host sister got in touch with me and said that her niece had applied to be an exchange student to the United States and that the exchange program was having a hard time finding families for her. She explained that her niece had applied twice and was not going to be able to come to the United States because this was her last possible year to go due to their age restrictions. So, I offered to host her and she came and lived in my home. Just a couple years ago I also hosted her brother. In the bigger picture sometimes we never know when we will experience the full and even unintended consequences of our actions. If I hadn't pursued going to Brazil and being an exchange student even after being rejected, none of this would have happened. Sometimes your actions come around in the most amazing ways, even decades later. As the saying goes, *"What goes around comes around."*

I want to suggest that Karma infinite. Everything that we say and do works like a drop of water ripples outward in a pond. These ripples overlap as our words, actions and events are constantly happening. The ramifications keep coming back to us, in one way or another, directly or indirectly. And why is that? Well, it's because we are all as one.

Oneness takes into account the realization that we affect one another because we are interconnected. Interconnectivity is something that's been important historically but we can even look at own industry. Look at what happened during the real estate bust, for example. During the boom, there were a lot of irresponsible lending practices and the result was a bust of enormous proportions. It affected all of us in the United States and abroad in significant ways.

When I think about interconnectivity, I think about some of my personal heroes in life—Martin Luther King, Gandhi and Steven Covey, to name a few. The following quote is from King's "I have a dream" speech: *"...for many of our white brothers, as evidenced by their presence here today, have come to realize that their destiny is tied up with our destiny and they've come to realize that their freedom is inextricably bound to our freedom... Whatever affects one directly, affects all indirectly."* I couldn't agree more. That's how connected we are. That's what the notion of oneness is. Keep in mind our oneness and interconnectivity as you interact with your customers every day.

Gandhi similarly states, *"Interdependence is and ought to be as much an ideal of the man as self-sufficiency. Man is a social being. Without interrelation with society he cannot realize his oneness with the universe or suppresses egotism. His social interdependence enables him to test his faith and prove himself as it has shown at the touchstone of reality."*

I'm going to suggest, though, that it's not as much a matter of faith as of empirical evidence. All you have to do is look around. Think about your relationships with your family members. If one person's in a funk then it sometimes brings everybody else down. Conversely, when somebody shares something that's joyful, can everybody else feel that joy? Absolutely! That's how connected we are.

The late Steven Covey sums this concept up really well in terms of the business environment. *"Independent thinking alone is not suited to interdependent reality. Independent people who do not have the maturity to think and act interdependently may be good individual producers, but they won't be good leaders or good team players. They're not coming from the paradigm of interdependence which is necessary to succeed in marriage and family or in an organizational reality."*

Karma shows us that what we put out comes back. The energy that we send out comes back to us in like kind and that we're all connected to each other. We need to be very cognizant of our actions. Another thing that you want to ask yourself is, "What is it that's driving me?" What is it that's driving your actions?

## Be Prepared

Once you know where you're going, you want to stay focused and determined on your goals and prepare for success. Your preparedness demonstrates your belief that your desired outcome is being realized. Not that it's *going* to be realized, that it is *being* realized! Demonstrate your belief.

One of my practices when I was a new home sales professional was that I always had 10 purchase agreements ready. Now, was I typically going to write 10 contracts in the day? Not usually, but I'll tell you one thing, I was prepared. I was open to it. I was ready for it. I would whip out one, could whip out two, could whip out three, no problem. Those of you on the front line, how many purchase agreements do you have ready, with the exception of the pages that you need to customize with customers' information, home site, lot number, floor plan, that sort of thing? You're not sitting there printing out all these pages. All the pages that can be printed ahead of time are printed and ready and in a packet to sign. You're only printing the last few pages that need to be specific to that person and home site. Being absolutely prepared for success demonstrates your belief to the universe that your desired outcome is being realized.

To have integrity with yourself is aligning your activities and your goals, ultimately, with your vision of yourself for your life. Mother Theresa said it beautifully: *"Be faithful in small things."* Believing in the small things demonstrates your belief when you act on them. It's in the details that your strength lies. That's where your power is. You've got the power to make all kinds of things happen. It doesn't happen around you. You've got to do something. Behave as if everything is coming together just as you expect. And yes, at one point, I did write ten contracts in one day.

## Abundant Thinking

Abundant thinking is the notion that there's enough for everybody, versus having a scarcity mentality. It is knowing that there is enough of everything for everyone. It's a true win-win-win mentality. Notice it's not just a win-win situation. This is because it's a win for the salesperson, it's a win for the customer, and it's a win for the company. It's a win for all parties involved. As we begin to think more abundantly, in the business environment rather than competing in terms of price, for example, we maintain our prices and we increase our service to customers. Why do we do that? We increase our service because service is infinite. The time for service never lacks. Contrarily, there is a time and place for price competition and incentives. But it's neither the time nor the place any longer. The market has hit bottom, virtually across the nation, and it is time to maximize our prices. In fact, in many markets, we need to so that we can actually afford the land that needs to be developed and built on.

Where you can compete, though, is in terms of service. Compare any two major stores, for example. You walk into one store and can't get help. There may not even be somebody at the cash register. You walk into next store and the sales associate is there to assist you. When you get down to it, there are a lot of commercial competitors offering night-and-day service. There may not be a perceptible price difference. What lacks in one is an abundance mentality. When a company ups its service game, it doesn't have to rely so much on having sales all the time.

A great example from my personal experience was with Zappos.com. A couple of years ago, I ordered a pair of shoes from the Zappos website. The shoes arrived and I was getting ready to wrap them up and I opened up the box and it was the right shoe, it was the right size, it was the wrong color. Zappos sent me the wrong colored shoes. I called the company immediately on its 24-hour 1-800 number. The representative at Zappos immediately apologized for the mistake and agreed to send me the right shoes. The second pair of shoes was overnighted to me without charge. The company instructed me to go ahead a return the first pair within couple weeks, excused me from paying the shipping, and then made me a VIP customer, which meant that I would receive free overnight shipping from Zappos.com for life! That was amazing customer service. The part I was most impressed with was that the company over-nighted the right pair of shoes to me without even receiving the wrong pair in return first. Zappos trusted me as a customer and, as a result, I trust that company to this day.

That type of service is how to maintain prices, or even raise prices, without continued increase in the amenity level. If you provide extraordinary, unparalleled customer service to your customers, you will see the results you want.

## Contribution

Contribution is the law of giving and receiving. What do you do to give back to the building industry? When I was in new home sales, I was a fundraiser for HomeAid. There was a point in my career that I felt like I wanted to give back to the industry that has given me so much. I called the president of our BIA and said I wanted to work with HomeAid, which is an organization that provides homes and shelters for people who are temporarily homeless. I was told the organization needed fundraisers, which was exactly what I had in mind.

Fundraising for HomeAid gave me a tremendous amount of joy. There is something amazing that comes back to you when you contribute on that level. Winston Churchill said it perfectly: *"We make a living by what we get. We make a life by what we give."* I believe it's important to give what's wanted or needed. Whatever you choose, if you choose to make a contribution in life, I really think that the Karmic results are something that's beyond what I can articulate. Give but don't necessarily do it for the recognition. Do it for a bigger picture, even if it's a "selfish" reason that you just want to feel good about yourself. Give without knowing where you're going to receive a benefit from or how it's going to come back to you. You most likely won't know what will come of it. Just trust and believe and know through your own experience that it does come back to you.

## Gratitude

Finally, I'd like to focus on gratitude. Those of you who are in sales and know what you are grateful for can and will attract more—more customers, more sales, and more results. Gratitude does attract more of what one wants. Be grateful for people and their contributions, their talents, their strengths, their actions. One of the best bosses I worked for always saw the best in others and it brought out the best in us. He trusted and empowered the people below him instead of trying to control and manipulate. He had a positive way of helping people beyond their weaknesses. I think it all started with seeing the best.

Gratitude opens your mind to possibilities. There are unlimited possibilities in life. Look at an adverse or challenging situation with gratitude and see another learning opportunity. We all come out bigger and better because of it. What's good and what you can be grateful for in any given situation expand the realm of possibilities. Gratitude opens your heart and your mind to what the possibilities are and that's how it will help you learn. Finally, in terms of your own business efforts, gratitude adds to the bottom line. It increases your productivity and the results because it grants you a positive perspective.

## Love

My final note is the power of love. To love what you do every day. Hopefully in this business you are doing what you love. Love what you do, do what you love, and to do it with love.

## ACKNOWLEGEMENTS

There are so many people that I need to thank. First, are all the sales mentors that I've had during my career. Other authors, especially those quoted and recognized in this book for sharing their energy and expertise and for sharing it with the world and me in particular. It's because of generous leaders like you that I had somebody in whose footsteps to follow. I am grateful to all the sales trainers who have touched my life including, Greg the owner of Swiss Colony and his two sales managers who also supported us in training. The woman at Boni trained me to sell facial lotion in fine department stores. From her I learned how to connect with a more refined clientele. Next, I am ever so grateful to the managers whose names I don't remember anymore, in the car business. From many of you, I learned how to aggressively close for the sale and to have the guts to ask people to buy more than once. It was through Volkswagen that I first learned how to methodically demonstrate a car which I was then able to apply to fax machines, copiers and homes. Tom Plendal from Canon USA taught me how to professionally approach big accounts. He was a super salesman! Mike Ferry taught me the questions to ask to get a listing and what questions to ask to access a seller's motivation to sell. His son, Matt Ferry taught me how to conduct cold calls.

I especially want to thank Tony Tonso for taking the time to really interview me for the job as a new home salesperson. He had a six page questionnaire provided by Bob Schultz. The interview took two hours but by the time we were done, I knew I wanted to work for him. He hired me green when no other builder would.

Continuing with my experience in new homes, I'd like to thank Charles Clarke III for BOLT Personality training and Marilyn Gardner for her enthusiastic support. She was the first person to allow me to assist in sales training and permitted me to share some of my inspirational favorites with other student salespeople. Thanks to Bob Schultz for his ABCs of New Home Sales. I used to listen to Bob's tapes over and over on my way to work. To the late Dr. Stephen R. Covey, I owe the sincerest and humblest gratitude. Covey's teachings in his *7 Habits of Highly Effective People* is, to this day, my all-time favorite book to turn to for sound advice on how to cope with any situation and to be a better person. He was my number one hero. Likewise, Martin Luther King Junior was my first inspiration as a teenager. In the eighth grade, I was so moved by his *"I have a dream"* speech during black history week that I knew that when I grew up I wanted to be a public speaker and make the world a better place. I'm also appreciative of Bonnie Alfriend for teaching the Certified Sales Professional class and Nikki Joy for making me laugh while I learned about the power and influence of the female buyer. I listened to her tapes over and over too.

I especially want to acknowledge my former boss, Alan Newman, for giving me great communities and allowing me to run with my ideas. I never felt held back by Alan. He always saw the best in others. He set an outstanding example and I have since realized that quality is the true sign of an outstanding leader.

Thanks to my sales partner, Fred Jacobs, for being a great partner on a competitive floor. He always kept me on my toes. I knew I couldn't let my follow up ball drop or he'd pick it up and sell my prospects and get the whole commission. He also professionally tolerated it when I sold his. Thanks for showing that a competitive floor does work and doesn't have to be cutthroat.

My repeat customer, and more importantly my friend, Johnny Comilang for telling me one day in my sales center that I should write a book. I never forgot his words. I appreciate his encouragement.

I'm also grateful to those who mystery shopped me. By your example, you permissioned me to take knowing thy competition to the unpopular extreme.

I am grateful to all the sales people at Beazer Homes who worked for me. We kicked butt during a challenging and sometimes depressing market. You all taught me to be a better leader and to constantly figure out how we could make more sales. You all worked hard, did an outstanding job and made me look good. We were a great team together.

I am also grateful to the late Brian Klemmer for creating Klemmer and Associates Personal Development and Leadership training. I met Brian at his book signing at a store in Corte Madera when his Compassionate Samurai was first published. He elaborated on the characteristic of Boldness. I'll never forget the story he told where the conclusion was that *"If you're not shaking, then you're not taking big enough risks."* The folks at K&A are truly committed to helping people get past the paradigms that hold them back from achieving their greatness.

I'd also like to thank all the builders who believed in me and hired me for consulting, training and mystery shopping. I am eternally grateful for your trust and confidence.

I want thank my mother for setting a great example in real estate, for encouraging me to pursue a career in sales and for convincing me to sell real estate and to go into new home sales. She's the one who suggested I apply at Beazer Homes.

I want to thank my dad for being extreme in his thinking and showing me how to think big. He piqued my interest in business, economics and commodities.

Finally, I want to thank Chris, for loving me. He also proof read the manuscript, puts my teachings into practice, and tells me I'm amazing.

Last I am eternally grateful for my son, Cayman. He is the son I always dreamed of and the greatest joy of my life. I am absolutely proud of him.

My success is the result of the teachings of all those before me. What's written in this book reflects the echoes of those who preceded me. As I shared in my self-introduction, I am purely a product of professional training. I hope you appreciate my contribution to our industry and trade for I have shared what I believe to be truthful about success in new home sales and my energy, enthusiasm, seriousness and best practices.

Thanks also to all of you who are committed to becoming exceptional salespeople. I am grateful for those who have attended my webinars, watched and liked my videos on YouTube and who have read and purchased this book. This book is for you!

# REFERENCES

Bettger, Frank. (1992). *How I Raised Myself from Failure to Success in Selling.* New Jersey: Touchstone.

Chapman, Gary. (1995). *The Five Love Languages: How to Express Heartfelt Commitment to Your Mate.* Chicago, IL: Northfield Publishing.

Coelho, Paulo (1988). *The Alchemist.* New York, NY: HarperTorch.

Covey, Stephen R. (2013). *The 7 Habits of Highly Effective People: Powerful Lessons in Personal Change* (25th edition). New York, NY: Simon & Schuster.

Doran, George. (1981). *There's a S.M.A.R.T. Way to Write Management's Goals and Objectives. Management Review.* 70(11), p. 35-36.

Gladwell, Malcolm. (2005). *Blink: The Power of Thinking without Thinking.* New York, NY: Back Bay Books, Little, Brown and Company.

Gladwell, Malcolm. (2000). *The Tipping Point: How Little Things Can Make a Big Difference.* New York, NY: Little, Brown and Company.

Klemmer, Brian. (2004). *If How-To's Were Enough We'd All Be Skinny Rich and Happy.* Tulsa, OK: Insight Publishing Inc.

Klemmer, Brian. (2008). *The Compassionate Samurai: Being Extraordinary in an Ordinary World.* United States: Hay House.

Rackham, Neil. (1988). *SPIN Selling.* New York, NY: McGraw-Hill Professional Publishing.

Siegel, Connie McClung. (1983). *Sales: The Fast Track for Women.* London, England: Macmillan Publishing Company, Inc.

Made in the USA
Middletown, DE
30 October 2014